Marius Albiez, Gerhard Banse, Kenyon C. Lindeman, Alexandra Quint (Eds.)

# Designing Sustainable Urban Futures

## Concepts and Practices from Different Countries

# Designing Sustainable Urban Futures

## Concepts and Practices from Different Countries

Edited by
Marius Albiez,
Gerhard Banse,
Kenyon C. Lindeman,
Alexandra Quint

KIT Scientific Publishing

**Impressum**

KIT Scientific Publishing

Karlsruher Institut für Technologie (KIT)
KIT Scientific Publishing
Straße am Forum 2
D-76131 Karlsruhe

KIT Scientific Publishing is a registered trademark of Karlsruhe Institute of Technology. Reprint using the book cover is not allowed.

www.ksp.kit.edu



Print on Demand 2016

ISBN 978-3-7315-0543-3
DOI 10.5445/KSP/1000055831

# Contents

# Introduction

*Marius Albiez, Gerhard Banse, Kenyon C. Lindeman, Alexandra Quint*

Urbanization and reurbanization are characteristic features of development in the early 21st century, a global megatrend. Cities, where over 50% of the world's population now live (and this share is increasing; cf. UN 2015), account for the most global economic performance, consumption of energy, greenhouse gas production, and amounts of waste produced. But on the other hand, cities also offer best opportunities for dealing with current challenges as "engines of innovations" and transformation processes in prior centuries. Urban actors can create synergies of people, resources, human and financial capital, and potential innovation skills and networks. So cities are both: responsible for and affected by global change. They pose not only significant risks but also provide great opportunities to advance sustainable development. The dense and compact city has the potential to be a sustainable and resource-saving living space when multifunctional structures, a well integrated transportation infrastructure network and democratic development processes are given. Sustainable urban futures require a focus on the needs of humans, environmental friendliness and health.

This book is based on contributions to the international symposium on "Sustainable Urban Development at Different Scales" organized by the Institute for Technology Assessment and Systems Analysis (ITAS) at the Karlsruhe Institute of Technology (KIT), Karlsruhe, Germany, in May 2014. The symposium took the global urbanization and reurbanization trend as an occasion to discuss cities as sustainable living spaces. The event "brought together experiences from theory and practice as well as different cultural and disciplinary perspectives on current issues of sustainable urban development at different scales and in different local contexts" (Quint/Albiez 2014, p. 116).

The symposium was held in cooperation with the Florida Institute of Technology, Melbourne, FL, U.S., and the Budapest University of Technology and Economics, Budapest, Hungary. This was the 10th symposium of the trans-Atlantic research initiative "Forum on Sustainable Technological Development in a Globalizing World" initiated in 2002 in Budapest.[1] Details on these past conferences are provided at the end of this introduction.

1 Cf. http://www.itas.fzk.de/tatup/041/itas-news.htm.

The conference examined several cross-cutting features of urban and institutional sustainability. The research highlighted examples from Europe, Asia, North and South America. Results suggest that geographic and socio-economic differences in urban sustainability can occur across continents and within. Complex systems interplay among economic, social and environmental sub-systems were evident in many case studies. Optimizing the communication of technical information between sometimes polarized stakeholders and government agencies can be central to measurable advances with sustainability challenges.

Examples from countries worldwide show that leadership in urban and regional sustainability has been advanced by universities and associated institutions. Such institutions along with the increasingly diverse and effective NGO community have collectively educated new sustainability leaders, provided proof-of-concept of applied projects, and through research and development, helped drive government and industry innovation.

In research and policy approaches, priority is often given to advances in sustainable development activities in urban and metropolitan regions. It is necessary to consider and address the most relevant problems, risk factors, and constraints including climate change, environmental pollution, resource scarcity, demographics and immigration dynamics, social inequality and fragmentation. Technical questions for problem solving include relevant socio-economic, institutional, and organizational aspects.

The increasing differentiation of urban space requires an intensive discussion of the challenges of its sustainable development at different scales. A growing number of megacities are in contrast to other cities in western societies. Additionally, the meaning of the local scale with its cultural and social specificities gains importance in the context of urban transformation (cf. Quint/Parodi 2014; Schnur 2014). This pushes forward the relevance of districts in research and development. All in all, spacial scales include those equal to or below that of the entire city and city region (meta level) with a focus on neighborhoods down to individual elements of the built city, e.g., buildings (meso level). Questions of assessment, community governance, environmental quality, housing provision and land use planning play a central role in the search for suitable conceptual and methodological approaches.

The needs and real living conditions of people can be well identified and analyzed at these intermediate, district scales. Elements of community, identity, commitment, participation, and solidarity are more tangible and easier to examine compared with the higher-scales of a city. Issues such as mobility, traditional supply systems, and interactions between different economic, technological, natural, and social sub-systems can be better analyzed and managed at this level. Therefore district-scales play an important role for urban transitions to more sustainable practices. Integrative approaches including the different dimensions of sustainability, diverse technical disciplines, and business and government sectors are essential to these studies.

The main objectives of the 10th symposium of the "Forum on Sustainable Technological Development in a Globalizing World" were to address the above areas of research on urban systems and their interrelations, to reflect on the different types and functions of district-scale issues, and to discuss previous experiences with practical implementation in the design and application of concepts, assessment methods, and actions towards more sustainable urban systems.

*****

This book is divided into four sections: Framework (1), Research and Development Processes (2), Opportunities and Challenges for Sustainable Cities (3), and Sustainable Universities (4). Sustainable Development is generally known as "development that meets the needs of the present without compromising the ability of future generations to meet their own needs" (WCED 1987, p. 41). An important element of this definition is inter- and intra-generational equity.

*Section One* deals with this temporal element in several manners: *Kerstin Gothe* focuses on the current challenges of sustainable development from the perspective of urban planning. *Armin Grunwald* discusses questions which are essential for shaping cities in the future. *Thomas Lützkendorf* and *Maria Balouktsi* give an overview of different types of Sustainable Assessment Systems for new and existing neighborhoods in Germany.

The focus of *Section Two* lies in research and development processes in realizing urban sustainable development. *Oliver Parodi, Marius Albiez, Sarah Meyer-Soylu* and *Colette Waitz* use transdisciplinary research approaches to examine the transformation of an existing district of the city of Karlsruhe, Germany, into a sustainable district. In this context, active participation and experiments in an Urban Transition Lab play major roles to foster urban sustainable development and generate transformational knowledge. The chapters by *Albert Geiger* and by *Ildiko Tulbure* emphasize the roles of national governments and city administrations in sustainable development and local citizen participation. *Appukuttan Damodaran's* and *Tanushree Haldar's* research on climate stress and unsustainable resource utilization systems in peri-urban villages in Bangalore shows the importance of locality, ecosystem management, and cultural aspects in sustainable development processes.

All over the world, city populations are increasing. Urban conditions like limited space and high population pressures, as well as imports of energy and goods, make cities vulnerable to ecological, societal and economic challenges multiplied by climate change, demographic change, and destruction of ecosystems (cf. Rees 2012, pp. 262–265). However, cities offer spaces for new progressive ideas and opportunities to foster urban sustainable development and resilience. In *Section Three*, these two sides of the same coin are faced from a European point of view. *Anja Szypulski* examines the potential of co-housing for sustainable neighborhood development and discusses both obstacles and possibilities. The chapter by *Sandra Huning* focuses on the importance of gender, class, ethnicity, and other categories of social differentiation in terms of ways that urban spaces can be used in equitable manners. *Freya Brandl's* work on converting existing flats into communal apartments, emphasizes the role of communal-living in the context of an ageing society. This approach can reduce costs, support energy efficiency and foster social exchange. It also fits in with other examples of the sharing economy.

Urban universities have been essential engines of innovation for centuries and can serve as models for theoretical and applied research into sustainability across disciplines. In *Section Four, Ingrid Hemmer* and *Peter Bagoly-Simó* discuss relationships among universities and sustainable development in Germany using the example of the Catholic University of Eichstätt-Ingolstadt. Finally, *Kenyon Lindeman* shares experiences from the U.S. in developing four-year academic programs in Sustainability Studies at Florida institute of Technology and the utility of systems science in helping students decompose complexity among highly interdisciplinary subjects. In addition, some primary issues that were examined during the symposium are summarized in a separate outlet (cf. Quint/Albiez 2014).

These chapters highlight examples from Germany, several other European countries, India, and the US. Geographic and socio-economic differences in urban sustainability can occur across continents and within. In some regions, urban planning is often focused on re-inventing older, existing cities, while elsewhere, planning can be focused on managing rapid growth in new cities. Complex system interplay among economic, social and environmental sub-systems were evident in many case studies. The history of urban planning is well-developed in Europe compared to some other areas and there is evidence that collective foresight in community planning may contribute to more proactive societal responses to emerging challenges such as climate change than in areas without long traditions of urban and regional planning.

Especially in Europe, at least two general trends in the field of urban sustainable development appeared to be present. There are community-based approaches by civil society organizations like the Transition Town movement and there are approaches to develop technological innovations to improve sustainable development by companies or research establishments (cf. Quint/Albiez 2014). Both trends are embedded in their own institutional or social structures and follow their own logic, but they should not be understood as two separate paths. We have to combine both strategies to develop participative, well-adjusted approaches to face different challenges and dilemmas. Usually, this combination does not occur without conflicts. Therefore, we have to consider different stakeholder interests and the ability to satisfy them. It is equally necessary to include specific local and cultural conditions: every society should decide on its understanding of sustainability and the way to realize it.

In this case, Urban Transition Labs (see chapter 2, Parodi et al.) are a new and very interesting approach because they fulfill various functions and they offer spaces to examine new societal and technological innovations to improve sustainable development in a defined urban environment. They also further reduce boundaries between scientists and non-academics. Given the challenges, experimentation and education are not enough. How will we deal with coastal mega-cities with increasing sea level rise? How can we stop the deterioration of global ecosystems? How can we prevent increasing social inequality and the unavoidable cascade effects? This book cannot answer all of these questions but we hope it will advance the development of applied solutions.

*****

This volume would not exist if the authors had not been willing to comply with the requests of the editors regarding deadlines and other specifications. Thank you very much for this. We would also like to thank *Georg B. Kaiser,* Hohen Neuendorf near Berlin, who was in charge of the "formal" harmonization and design of this volume, *Katja Saar,* Karlsruhe, for the graphic layout, and *KIT Scientific Publishing,* Karlsruhe, for printing. In the U.S, we would like to thank *Gordon Nelson* for his leadership, *Siemens AG* for financial support, *Morgan Wilson* for data inputs, and *Bryan Lindeman* and *Beth Schoppaul* for assisting text reviews. Last but not least, the editors owe their thanks to *Jürgen Kopfmüller* and *Oliver Parodi* from ITAS for their conceptual and to ITAS and the KIT Focus Project on Humans and Technology for their financial support which was essential for both the symposium and the printing of this volume.

The editors would also like to express their hope that more applied scientific efforts on the issues examined here will follow, with new, societally important perspectives and applications. We are hopeful this work will exist not only as "book knowledge", but will also soon be reflected in measureable increases towards more sustainable practices at all scales.

## A Short History of these Conferences

Two universities, Florida Institute of Technology (Florida Tech) located in Melbourne, Florida, and the Budapest University of Technology and Economics (BME) have been cooperating since September 2001, supported by a U.S. State Department CUAP Grant for three years on environmental protection and environmentally sustainable technologies. The then existing Department of Innovation Studies and History of Technology at BME also had a long period of prior cooperation with the Institute of Technology Assessment and Systems Analysis (ITAS) at the (former) Research Center of Karlsruhe (Forschungszentrum Karlsruhe – FZK), now the Karlsruhe Institute of Technology (KIT). When BME and Florida Tech personnel met in June 2002 to conduct a

"Sustainable Tourism" workshop with participants from ITAS, they discussed the idea to initiate and develop a forum devoted to assessing how technological development can be made sustainable. The decision was made that these institutions would try to develop and realize international workshops devoted to this goal in Hungary, Germany and the U.S., alternating if possible. The resulting workshops were:

- 2003: "Rationality in an Uncertain World", Budapest, Hungary, December 4–6;
- 2005: "Sustainability's New Age, Preservation & Planning (SNAP)", Melbourne/FL, U.S., February 2l–23;
- 2005: "Converging Technologies – Promises and Challenges", Budapest, Hungary, December 8–10;
- 2007: "Sustainable Pathways: New Research and Practices", Melbourne/FL, U.S., March 6–7;
- 2007: "Foresight, Roadmapping, and Governance", Budapest, Hungary, December 7–8;
- 2009: "Sustainability 2009: The Next Horizon", Melbourne/FL, U.S., March 3–4;
- 2010: "Sustainability 2010: The Cultural Dimension", Berlin, Germany, June 9–12;
- 2011: "Sustainability 2011: Is It Worth It?", Melbourne/FL, U.S., March 8–9;
- 2012: "Regional Aspects of Sustainability", Eger, Hungary, June 7–9.

Published materials of the earlier conferences include (in chronological order):

- Nelson, G.; Hronszky, I. (eds.): How Science Can Support Environmental Protection? Florida tech-BME Partnership Programme Yearbook 2003. Budapest 2003
- Nelson, G.; Hronszky, I. (eds.): Science Supporting Environmental Protection. Budapest 2004
- Banse, G.; Hronszky, I.; Nelson, G. (eds.): Rationality in an Uncertain World. Berlin 2005
- Nelson, G.; Hronszky, I. (eds.): Environmental Studies. Implications for Sustainability. Budapest 2005
- Banse, G.; Grunwald, A.; Hronszky, I.; Nelson, G. (eds.): Assessing Societal Implications of Converging Technological Development. Berlin 2007
- Hronszky, I.; Nelson, G. (eds.): An International Forum on Sustainability. Budapest 2008
- Nelson, G. L.; Hronszky, I. (eds.): Sustainability 2009: The Next Horizon. Melville, NY 2009 (AIP Conference Proceedings, Vol. 1157)
- Banse, G.; Nelson, G. L.; Parodi, O. (eds.): Sustainable Development – The Cultural Perspective. Concepts – Aspects – Examples. Berlin 2011
- Banse, G.; Grunwald, A.; Hronszky, I.; Nelson, G. L. (eds.): On Prospective Technology Studies. Karlsruhe 2011 (KIT Scientific Reports 7599)

– Periodica Oeconomica 2012. Research Papers from the Field of Economic Science. Special Issue on the Regional Aspects of Sustainability. – URL: http://www.gti.ektf.hu/PO2012.html

## References

Quint, A.; Albiez, M. (2014): Sustainable Cities: Challenges and Opportunities at Different Scales. Report from the International Conference "Sustainability 2014: Future Urban Development at Different Scales". Karlsruhe, Germany, May 7–9, 2014. In: TATuP – Technikfolgenabschätzung. Theorie und Praxis, Vol. 23 (2014), No. 3 (November), pp. 116–118

Quint, A.; Parodi, O. (2014): Die europäische Stadt. Wege zur Nachhaltigkeit. In: Verantwortung Zukunft No. 2, pp. 42–46 (in German)

Rees, W. (2012): Cities as Dissipative Structures: Global Change and the Vulnerability of Urban Civilization. In Weinstein, M. P.; Turner, E. T. (eds.): Sustainability Science. The Emerging Paradigm and the Urban Environment. New York a.o.p., pp. 247–273

Schnur, O. (2014): Renaissance des Lokalen – Quartiere im Fokus von Wissenschaft und Politik. In: Ministerium für Bauen, Wohnen, Stadtentwicklung und Verkehr des Landes NRW (ed.): Bericht zur Stadtentwicklung 2013 – Quartiere im Fokus. Düsseldorf, pp. 6–10 (in German)

WCED – World Commission on Environment and Development (1987): Report of the World Commission on Environment and Development: Our Common Future (Brundtland Report). Oxford

UN – United Nations (2015): World Urbanization Prospects. The 2014 Revision. New York (UN, Department of Economic and Social Affairs, Population Division). – URL: http://esa.un.org/unpd/wup/Publications/Files/WUP2014-Report.pdf

## 1. Framework

# The Human in the City of the Future

## The Challenge of Shaping Future Urban Contexts

*Armin Grunwald*

## 1 The Human and the City in Historical Terms

"The future of humanity lies in cities", former Secretary General of the United Nations, Kofi Annan, once said. But maybe this is the way it has always been since the early days of advanced human civilization: A large part of human history is the history of humans in cities. Cities as locations of maximum population concentration were equally fascinating and provocative through the ages: the concentration of power, wealth, education, and creativity on one hand, of poverty, crime, social problems, and hunger for resources on the other. Cities do not balance, they polarize – and this is not only the key to their success, but also a way to express their ambivalence. The concern that the human or humanity might get lost in the city is not new:

– even biblical Babel was known as a symbol for human arrogance which results in failure;
– Fritz Lang's film *Metropolis* (1926) describes the utopian city as an elitist dictatorship per a randomly manipulable mass;
– the film "Berlin: Symphony of a Metropolis" (1927) also predominantly shows humans as a mass, e.g. on their way to work, by analogy with a cattle drive in agriculture; human individuality seems to have disappeared.

However, history seems to confirm the positive side of ambivalence. Cities remain highly attractive and it is not difficult to predict that this will also hold true in the future. Global trends in recent decades speak for themselves: the share of people living in cities is steadily growing. Futurologists agree: the future belongs to the cities.

Nevertheless, I want to water down the wine of pompous promises here. We do not really know that much about the future as we are sometimes made to believe. The fact that we currently experience clear trends towards the densification of cities, world-wide urbanization, and mega-urbanization does not imply that this trend will continue for decades. Just one example from the past: in the 1970s the "emptying of the cities", the suburbanization or escape to the little house in the countryside was a real issue in Germany. The slow death of cities was lamented; especially since the creative and the educated were leaving the cities and only the proletariat and the elderly were left. And these were not only figments of concerned researchers, these predictions were backed by the reality at that time. Suburbanization was a *real* trend, not an invented one. However, it turned out differently. The fact remains that future knowledge in principle is epistemologically precarious (cf. Grunwald 2013).

Also other expectations for the future did not occur. It was expected, for example, that the Internet would end the separation of the rural periphery from urban centers; after all, the Internet – and today all other mobile technologies would be included – provides access to global sources of information and possibilities of participation, irrespective of the place of residence. This effect exists – but there seem to be other, more potent effects. The attractiveness of today's condensed cities with their physical concentration of humans is definitely stronger than the Internet's power to overcome space.

## 2 Shaping the Urban Future Instead of Predicting It

The message of these two examples is clear: we should not overestimate current trends. Even though urbanization is in full swing at the moment, it is just a trend and not a law of nature – and trends can change.

However, we want to refer specifically to humans in the city of the future here. This was not always the first priority. Just think of the notorious "automotive city", a guiding principle in the time of the German economic miracle. Not the human but the car was the focus of the city of the future at that time. Or the architecture of huge concrete estates which resemble battery cages (sorry!). Numerous models and plans of past decades reduced the human to a minor character in the cities. Cities were partly considered and planned as functional infrastructures, where humans were only allocated certain roles. To exaggerate it: humans were sometimes downgraded to some sort of "terminal equipment" of a systemic infrastructure.

Countermovements were inevitable. In line with the well-known Friedrich Hölderlin quote: "But where the danger is, also grows the saving power". A new form of public spirit arose, the citizens were no longer willing to be subject to the plans of others, but claimed their right to participate and got – and still are – involved, for example, for a "sustainable urbanity". This observation of movement and countermovement seems to be symptomatic – and goes with the above-mentioned criticism of too much prophecy.

So let us assume, as mentioned before, that we do not know the city of the future. Let us be suspicious of trend analysts and futurologists who are convinced that they already know everything at this stage. Instead, let us not consider the development of tomorrow's city as some kind of inevitable fate or law of nature, but as something we can help to shape. This would change the role of the human being in the city of the future – no longer like that in the Delphic Oracle or Richard Wagner's Twilight of the Gods, where the Norns ask: "Do you know what will become of it?"

Instead, we reverse the question: how do we picture the human being – us – in the city of the future? Which expectations and fears do we have and what can we do to realize these expectations and make sure that these fears do not come true? This is a planning perspective and not a prophetic one. In this perspective, we do not assign the development of the city of the future to its own dynamics, dark forces or laws of nature, which might allow prognoses but, apart from that, only adapt to what is said to come anyhow. Instead, we take ourselves up on our promise and assume responsibility for the city of the future and the human's role within. Within this perspective, we should look for areas of conflict or problematic trends, but also for opportunities and new possibilities; for movements and countermovements, for wishes and visions. We should explore the options of how the city of the future could and also should look like (note: the singular is quite misleading here since we have to assume a large plurality of cities of the future). And we should not ask how the human being will appear in it, but rather: which kind of development of the role of the human in the city do we *want and strive for*? It is just a triviality, but one that is nevertheless often forgotten: cities are there for the humans, not the humans for the cities.

## 3 Challenges and Pathways to Shaping Urban Futures – Open Questions

So I would now like to come to the questions that are essential for shaping the cities of tomorrow and the role of the human beings within, or at least those questions that I consider essential:

– *The question of the city resident's relation to nature:* City and nature are regarded as opposites, the city as downright counter-nature. However, there are countermovements, e.g. "urban gardening". Does this only mean taking a share of rural romance into the city or does it imply a new form of awareness of nature of the city residents?
– *The question of sustainability:* Cities have a hunger for resources and activate vast material flows of water, food, energy, feedstock and other materials, all at the expense of the surrounding areas. How can we create stable and fair relations between the city and its surroundings, especially in megacities (cf. Yanarella/Levins 2011)?
– *The question of exclusion and inclusion:* Who gets access to the resources of the city and who is barred? Which kind of governance can allow for the best possible inclusion? Which methods of participation can allow for a democratic partnership of the humans in the city of the future? How are freedom and authority balanced?

- *The question of urbanity:* The European history of the city gave birth to urban visions – Athens, Siena, and Florence represent certain models of human coexistence in a cultural collective. Urbanity is more than living in an urban agglomeration. Are these visions of the city and the humans in the city taken into account in the plans for the future?
- *The question of diversity:* Cities of the future will be characterized – like today's cities – by an extreme diversity: Scandinavian cities, luxury cities on the Persian Gulf, South American cities full of contrasts, the lively chaos of many African cities, authoritarian cities in South East Asia – this variety shows how options for shaping future cities depend on the context. It is not about the human in the city of the future, but about a large variety.
- *The question of the relationship between humans and technology:* This question influenced the image of the human in the modern city long before Fritz Lang's "*Metropolis*". Infrastructures are an especially important topic. They are omnipresent in our cities and determine their rhythm of life. The question of whether the human being is the designer and gears the infrastructures to the standards of human needs or whether humans are forced to adapt themselves to infrastructures designed to meet technological, economic, or political requirements still seems to be unanswered.
- *The question of human individuality:* Urbanization and mega-urbanization do challenge the ideal of individuality. To what extent can this ideal be maintained or even developed further and can we counter tendencies of human collectivization? This applies especially to digital connectivity which, on the one hand, opens up new ways to keep our individuality and establish individual networks, but, on the other hand, fosters collectivization by adjusting to digital infrastructures.

# 4 Conclusion

Cities are places of contradiction and for that very reason are also focal points of creativity and places for experimentation. What these contradictions will look like, how they will be considered in decisions on future development and which forces will prevail cannot be predicted; it remains to be seen, but should also and above all be actively influenced. The human in the city of the future is not the product of laws of nature, but is the result of developments in which we can participate today.

# References

Grunwald, A. (2013): Der prekäre Status von Zukunftswissen zwischen hoher praktischer Relevanz und drohender Beliebigkeit. In: Banse, G.; Hauser, R.; Machleidt, P.; Parodi, O. (Hg.): Von der Informations- zur Wissensgesellschaft. e-Society – e-Partizipation – e-Identität. Berlin, S. 343–360

Yanarella, E. J.; Levine, R. S. (2011): The City as Fulcrum of Global Sustainability. London/New York

# Current Challenges of Sustainable Urban Development

*Kerstin Gothe*

This article focuses on the sustainable development of urban spaces and the challenges from the perspective of an urban planner who is interested in a particular district for analysis, assessment and action. As has been extensively discussed, there are three challenges of urban development and strategies to address them.

## 1 The Context of this Article

(1) Resources and energy supplies are limited. Cities can be seen not only as huge raw material deposits, but also as deposits of other features including water, energy, etc. (e.g., "grey energy"). There are several strategies to reduce these material flows: the principles of Reduce, Re-use, Recycle or Cradle to Cradle approaches being the most fundamental ones.

(2) Urban agglomerations are made more and more vulnerable by extreme climate occurrences (heat stress, storms, floods, or droughts). The overall focus must therefore be placed on developing strategies aiming to make cities more resilient by adapting to climate change. The concept of "green and sustainable cities" represents a valuable opportunity to achieve an increased urban resilience and also to improve the quality of life of residents. Cities must be strategically protected and improved.

(3) Urban regeneration needs to be managed and financed – this is the key to achieve the first two strategies. Stakeholders must be included in this process. Conflicting goals, i.e., between competing uses of limited resources, have to be solved as has historically been the case with cities. Today urban citizens have more opportunities than ever to be involved in decisions that affect their daily lives and environment (cf. BMBF 2015).

Strategies for "integrated urban governance" intending to find holistic and interdisciplinary solutions to existing challenges have to be found. New forms of cooperation and financing are necessary and technical solutions must be embedded in societal contexts. The "Quarter of the Future" and the activities of the ITAS (Institute for

Technology Assessment and Systems Analysis) are working on these questions, as well as urban planners such as those in Karlsruhe, to further the discussion of the spatial vision for the city (cf. SPAK 2015).

# 2 Actual Trends with Influence on the Development of Cities

But there are not only difficulties: we can we also identify actual trends that help to solve these problems:

1. The renaissance of the urban lifestyle or re-urbanisation;
2. The multimodality and changes in mobility patterns: the trend to organise daily life with different means of transportation, even without a car.

I want to build on these trends as a basis for developing a new trend: the rise of the Interactive City, with particular reference to the concept of the "Sharing City", presenting emerging trends in Germany as well as in the international context using examples from Seoul, South Korea.

## 2.1 The Renaissance of the Urban Lifestyle, or Re-Urbanisation

In Germany life in cities is becoming more attractive – this is true for big cities as well as for smaller cities, which serve as regional centres. In light of demographic change, new urban lifestyles and cultural and creative industries contributing to re-urbanisation can be identified:

- *Demographic change:* Elderly populations are growing and the number of single and two person households is increasing. Younger people flock to the cities for educational reasons and often end up staying.
- *New urban lifestyles:* The urban lifestyle is increasingly attractive even for families. The role of women in society has changed: for example, women stay employed even when their children are small. The ever-expanding local urban supply of health, culture, childcare, education and entertainment services support changes in family patterns. Working parents follow strict time regimes and they now prefer shorter commutes to work places. Many people may no longer rely on a car.
- *Cultural and creative industries and a knowledge-based service economy* in the cities are drivers of economic growth resulting from:
  - post-industrial values: people work more flexibly, independent of time and place;
  - new working conditions: conjunctions/intersections of work and private life;

- short-term employment relationships: therefore it is important to have access to labour-markets (cf. Kunzmann 2012).

- *Urban life becomes more attractive:*
  - urban lifestyle/"urban age": "urban" and "metro" are becoming fashionable trends;
  - inner city living is seen as an alternative to single house with a garden (cf. Herfert/Osterhage 2012);
  - a great variety of housing typologies is emerging as well as the desire for events, urban atmosphere and new forms of sociability (cf. Kunzmann 2012).

The urban renaissance and re-urbanisation will conceivably remain one of the dominant leading trends.

As in many European and American cities, the growth of Germany's cities was connected for decades to suburbanisation: the suburbs grew faster than the city. Private households, but also industrial, retail and service businesses withdrew to the edge of the city or beyond. Since 2000 there has been a trend reversal towards re-urbanisation (cf. Herfert/Osterhage 2012, p. 95).

Re-urbanization can be described statistically: the growth of the surrounding region of the cities slows, and the core of the city grows faster than the surrounding region, both in terms of households and employment opportunities. The city core is often revitalised through private and public building investments ("Urban Renaissance"). Conversions and brownfield developments offer new construction opportunities.

Since 2004 inner city populations in Germany have been increasing, much more than in suburban areas. Very few Western German city regions (Reutlingen, Lübeck) continue to show suburban growth and dwindling city centres. Re-urbanisation is mainly based on migration gains of the city centres (cf. Herfert/Osterhage 2012, pp. 100ff.).

However, re-urbanisation presents itself differently in the various parts of Germany:

- Type I (example: Munich) – *relative centralisation:* The population has grown significantly in the city core and only slightly in the region.
- Type II (example: Düsseldorf) – *absolute centralisation:* The population has grown in the city core and decreased in the region.
- Type III (example: Kassel) – *relative centralisation:* The population in the city core has decreased, but less so than in the region.
- Type IV (example: Wilhelmshaven) – *deurbanisation:* People migrate to more prosperous city regions; population in the city core continues to decrease faster than in the region (cf. Herfert/Osterhage 2012, p. 100).

Re-urbanisation in Eastern Germany (type III) is predominantly caused by interregional migrations which have taken place since 2005. The population stays in the inner cities instead of moving away, there is a population influx from inside the federal state.

## 2.2 The Decline of Car Traffic, Multimodality

For the first time in the history of motorisation the number of cars is declining. This presents new opportunities for urban spaces and the reduction of energy consumption and $CO_2$ (carbon dioxide) emissions.

Each mode of transport has its own ideal urban range, e.g. pedestrians up to one kilometre, cyclists up to three kilometres. Multimodal users know how to combine them. Instead of a universally applicable solution like a car, multiple means of transport are combined to complement each other's strengths. Younger people especially have been using multimodal transportation in recent years, because new forms of mobility are introduced and supported financially by way of student ticket prices, and because the car is less of a status symbol than it once was; also, shared or rental cars are easy accessible; and the car is becoming less attractive for commuting and long-distance travel. Multimodal behaviour requires complex strategies and planning routes in advance. Smartphones and mobile internet greatly support this.

The new multimodals organise their life without their own car. Multimodality can be supported by simplifying the switching of modes (e.g. bicycle and tram) and offers like call-a-bike, car sharing or Car2Go, combined with attractively positioned, clearly visible parking options for shared vehicles (cf. Chlond 2013; Streit et al. 2014).

# 3 Thinking about the Role of the "Sharing City" or "Interactive City"

The Interactive City is mostly discussed in the context of the link between urban infrastructures that until now typically operated separately. Linking infrastructures brings new opportunities: communications technology in "smart cities" link mobility, energy supply (power, gas, water and heating), sewage, as well as waste management.

I want to focus on the following questions: Can a "sharing culture" make cities more sustainable? Do sharing cities find new ways of using urban space? Are they changing relationships with private-space resources? Are they changing social urban life?

The idea of sharing is not new. "Parks and green spaces in cities have always existed as shared spaces. Libraries share books. Public transport is a shared method for getting around. But the advent of digital communications facilitates sharing in a way never seen before" (Childs 2014). The sharing city gets fresh impulses by new technological developments such as 3D printing, robotics, and the continued expansion of the digital economy.

Examples of sharing initiatives include: car-sharing, bike-sharing, shared housing, shared jobs, shared offices, tool sharing, shared ownership of energy generation, local currencies, shared green space for relaxation or growing food, even shared dogs. The goal of the Sharing City is to create jobs or to increase incomes, to address environmental issues, to reduce unnecessary consumption and waste, and to recover trust-based relationships between people.

Sharing could make the difference *for the urban space*, because it leads to increased resource efficiency, it makes better use of the limited capacity of space and even raises money for urban regeneration projects. Furthermore, strategic benefits *for the society* could flow from the development of a Sharing City, because it creates active communities and social cohesion, it helps provide support for the weakest in society and enables them to access services and opportunities that would otherwise be unavailable to them. Sharing can also *foster technological development*, because it grabs hold of technological developments and uses them for the common good; it builds a community of people who can collaborate in further developing and shape them; it creates a culture of innovation and can also help keep economies local, making them more resilient to global change. In many cases sharing has more than one purpose (cf. Childs 2014).

# 4 Practice of Sharing City-Projects

In this section, I want to characterize some examples of Sharing City-Projects, the first four examples are in Germany, the latter from abroad.

- *Damage reporter (Mängelmelder)* is a website and application for smartphones that reports requests from users such as repairing a bench in the city and gives feedback to the user about the repair.[1]
- *Void reporter (Leerstandsmelder)* is a website for reporting unused properties in cities with additional information. It delivers services about articles of related themes or events involving unused properties. It started in the city of Hamburg 2011 from initiatives under the architect Michael Ziehl. By 2013 it had spread to thirteen German cities.[2]
- *New uses for private and public properties: "BetweenTimeCentral-Office Bremen" (ZwischenZeitZentrale Bremen):* The users search suitable properties for temporary uses and provide advice for property owners, develop concepts with other users and follow the projects. A win-win situation can occur for all engaged parties: the users obtain rooms for a low price, the houses are used and maintained, and vandalism is avoided. It is run through "Autonomes Architektur Atelier GbR (Gesellschaft bürgerlichen Rechts, Society of Civic Rights)".

1 Cf. http://www.mängelmelder.de [11.12.2013].
2 Cf. http://www.leerstandsmelder.de [11.12.201].

- *New uses for private and public properties: "Temporary Space corporation" (Raum auf Zeit)* was founded in 2006 and develops temporary use concepts for offices and atelier flats for start-ups in favourable locations in good condition. The target objects are business offices in central locations which have stood empty for the short or long term due to their condition.[3]
- *Bringing up new ideas for cities financed by crowd-funding: Spacehive.* This platform was developed by Chris Gourlay in London in 2011. It organises crowdfunding for civic projects in communities: local citizens share their ideas to improve their community, such as organizing quality green spaces, new sports infrastructure or a thorough extension of a main street. "Design professionals" propose the project ideas to attract enough crowdfunding directly to the municipality.

  *An example:* Conversion of a concrete flyover into an urban park for Liverpool: "a vibrant place full of life, trees, shops, exhibitions & joy". "We don't feel it's right to spend £ 3-4 million (for the demolition of the flyover) and see nothing in return, so we used our design talent to propose something different."[4] The idea is to create "a new way for pedestrians and cyclists to connect to the heritage quarter of the city, to develop a programme of live cultural events in partnership with the many creative agencies in the city and to provide spaces for small independent businesses to develop and trade." They are hoping to create a new trust to manage and maintain the structure.

- *Intensification of parking space usage (Park IT):* This website and application for smartphones were developed in 2011 from a collaboration between Startup@UZH (University of Zürich), the Schweizer Bundesbahn (Swiss Federal Railways) and private firms. It is an interactive platform that allows Swiss citizens to share private parking lots. The participants pay monthly for their parking over smartphones with a credit card.[5]
- *New uses for Parking Places: Parklets in San Francisco.* This project has been ongoing since 2009, initiated from the San Francisco Planning Department in the USA. It is part of the Pavement to Parks program. Public and private actors are working together: merchants, community organizations or residents submit a proposal and get a permit for a parklet, if possible. The program facilitates the conversion of utilitarian spaces in the street into publicly accessible open spaces. Its aims are to improve the aesthetics of the streetscape, to find economic solutions for creating more public open space, to foster vitality and activity for the streets, and to support the diversity and creativity of the people. The larger purpose is to encourage walking and biking to strengthen the communities, and to support local

3 Cf. http://www.raumaufzeit.de [12.12.2013].
4 Cf. https://spacehive.com/theflyoverliverpool [05.05.2014].
5 Cf. https://www.facebook.com/parkit.ch/ [11.12.2015].

business communities. Amenities like seating, gardens and art are provided. Within three years (from 2010 to 2013) 38 parklets have been installed (cf. SFPD 2013).

- *Flexibility and regulations for underutilized spaces: Space Noah and Dr. Noah Dental Clinic in Seoul, South Korea.* Space Noah was a preliminary project that created new co-working space and opened in December 2012.[6] Space Cloud converted an empty property in inner-city Seoul into a multi-use space, providing co-working spaces such as seminar rooms, a media lab, and a connecting hall with café facilities. The Space Cloud service was launched due to the high demand for multi-use spaces.[7] The supply and demand for space are connected according to desired uses, rent prices and space capacities.
- *Social interconnections in neighbourhoods: Knock Knock Library in Seoul.* The idea is to provide a large number of bedtime books for toddlers and babies in every household through organising a library system in a neighbourhood. The project applies the self-contained character of "Tanji", using web-based and phone platforms for intercommunication. The benefits include the exchange of knowledge among early youth such as hand skills (e.g., wrapping books or making ribbons) or learning foreign languages.[8]

# 5 Discussion of the Sharing City concept in Seoul

In this last section, I summarize some thoughts about the impact of the Sharing City in Seoul and the expectations for a more sustainable city.

Challenges faced by the City of Seoul are overpopulation and the impacts of urbanisation: therefore the city must confront the lack of housing, transportation and parking shortages, pollution, and resource overuse. Mayor Park Won-soon has a history of social activism and innovative problem-solving and brought the idea of the Sharing City from San Francisco to Seoul. While it was more a grassroots movement in San Francisco, the Seoul Metropolitan Government is actively working to create a culture of sharing (for the following cf. Johnson 2014).

Seoul supports the Sharing City through the following activities:

- *Encouragement and nurturing of sharing:* Sharing enterprises are promoted citywide in order to strengthen the public's perception of the Sharing City as something that crosses demographic boundaries.
- *Development and implementation of a strategic vision:* A comprehensive plan "encompasses public awareness, business incubation, new regulation, and mobili-

6 Cf. http://www.spacenoah.net [01.04.2014].
7 Cf. http://www.spacecloud.kr [11.12.2013].
8 Cf. http://www.knocklibrary.org [11.12.2013].

zation of the city's underutilized assets" – sharing non-profits and corporations are vetted and designated. "By putting the city's stamp of approval on select sharing services, the city builds the public's trust in the sharing economy."

- *Removal of barriers to the development of sharing:* Officials are also working to correct obstructive statutes or systems, and facilitate communication between sharing enterprises and the central government. The Social Innovation Division will handle sharing-related civilian proposals and requests.
- *Investment in sharing enterprises:* The City of Seoul subsidizes "the expenses of 10 sharing enterprises with 250 million won (U.S. $ 240,000; EUR 180,000). Providing 10 sharing enterprises with the funding to either launch or scale up their platform gives the enterprises a bit of financial breathing room to focus on building or enhancing their service. [...] Incubating approximately 20 sharing startups with office space, consultation, and subsidies. Providing space, guidance and some funding to sharing startups will allow businesses to take their service to the next level and the city to support innovative ideas and thinkers" (Johnson 2014).
- *Promotion of the Sharing City:* Branding Seoul as one of the great cities for sharing is a powerful way to attract international attention, accelerate the city's sharing economy and position the city as a forward-thinking hub of innovation. "Creating a Seoul Sharing Promotion Committee made up of representatives from a variety of sectors including academic, legal, press, welfare, transportation and more. Having a team of representatives from numerous sectors who are all on board with the Sharing City plan is a good way to extend the reach of the sharing economy, make sure that it's being promoted appropriately in the various sectors and ensure that sharing is part of the discussion when decisions within those sectors are being made." Creating an International Sharing City Conference "further brands Seoul as an innovative locale and provides other municipalities from around the world a chance to see a sharing city plan in action" (Johnson 2014).

But a sharing economy cannot be imposed upon a city. Participation in developing, enacting and owning the plan is as obvious as it is critical. And cities themselves need significant autonomy from national governments to develop this agenda. "Building a sharing economy is a strategic response to actual challenges, turning them around and using them as an opportunity to build a socially cohesive and environmentally sustainable future" (Johnson 2014). The future will show whether sharing economies are important for the usage of urban space, and whether they are changing the relationships among private space-resources and urban social life.

We will see whether sharing economies will have full opportunities to improve prospects for sustainable urban development.

## References


BMBF – Bundesministerium für Bildung und Forschung (ed.) (2015): Die Zukunftsstadt – $CO_2$-neutral, energie-/ressourceneffizient, klimaangepasst und sozial. Langfassung der Strategischen Forschungs- und Innovationsagenda (FINA). Berlin (BMBF, Referat Nachhaltigkeit, Klima, Energie) (in German)

Childs, M. (2014): Seoul: Can a "Sharing Culture" Make Cities More Sustainable? – URL: http://www.sustainablecities.eu/local-stories/seoul-city/ [05.05.2014]

Chlond, B. (2013): Multimodal unterwegs – Überlegungen für eine gesamtheitliche Planung unseres Verkehrssystems. Lecture. Karlsruhe (Institut für Verkehrswesen am KIT) (non-published)

Herfert, G.; Osterhage, F. (2012): Wohnen in der Stadt: Gibt es eine Trendwende zur Reurbanisierung? In: Brake, K.; Herfert, G. (eds.): Reurbanisierung. Materialität und Diskurs in Deutschland. Wiesbaden, pp. 86–112 (in German)

Johnson, C. (2014): Is Seoul the Next Great Sharing City? – URL: http://ourworld.unu.edu/en/is-seoul-the-next-great-sharing-city [05.05.2014]

Kunzmann, K. (2012): Das urbane Pentagon von Konsum, Tourismus, Kultur, Wissen und Kreativwirtschaft. In: Brake, K.; Herfert, G. (eds.): Reurbanisierung. Materialität und Diskurs in Deutschland. Wiesbaden, pp. 151–163 (in German)

SFPD – San Francisco Planning Department (2013): Parklet Manual. Version 1.0. San Francisco/CA

SPAK – Stadtplanungsamt Karlsruhe (ed.) (2015): Auf dem Weg zum Räumlichen Leitbild Karlsruhe. Karlsruhe (in German)

Streit, T.; Chlond, B.; Weiß, C.; Vortisch, P. (2014): Alltagsmobilität und Fahrleistung. In: Deutsches Mobilitätspanel (MOP) – Bericht 2013/14. – URL: http://www.researchgate.net/profile/Bastian_Chlond/publications [05.05.2015] (in German)

# Sustainability Assessment Systems for New and Existing Neighbourhoods

*Thomas Lützkendorf, Maria Balouktsi*

## 1 Starting Points

When it comes to analysis of issues associated with the implementation of sustainability in the construction sector, an increasing focus on planning, management and assessment of the sustainability of human settlements (including urban districts and neighbourhoods) is noticeable. This issue is currently approached from two standpoints. On one hand, sustainability oriented urban development is usually part of national sustainability strategies; this is the case in Germany (cf. FGG 2002, p. 17). The necessary planning, management and assessment of sustainable urban development is a response to the growing importance of cities and the dramatic increase in their populations compared to the global population. Considering that the influence and control of sustainable urban development is a complex task, one approach is to subdivide the "city" system into smaller units and to involve local stakeholders in the development of these units, not only as people affected by this phenomenon, but also as actors or co-creators. This leads, among other results, to active engagement with the issue of sustainable neighbourhood development. This concept is built on the traditions of the Local Agenda 21 (cf. Keating 1993).

On the other hand, an intensive examination of the planning, management and assessment of the sustainability of individual buildings has been taking place over the last years. This movement has resulted in the development of several building sustainability assessment and certification systems (cf. Ebert et al. 2011, pp. 30-75). To respond to the need for addressing complex issues related to groups of buildings and neighbourhoods (e.g. optimal energy supply design, design of outdoor space and environment), there are attempts around the globe to expand the boundaries of these systems.

It is clear that the neighbourhood can be approached as the object of assessment both from the point of view of sustainable urban development and in terms of the further development and adaptation of sustainability assessment methods and tools for individual buildings including the urban scale. This paper examines which specific features a) characterise the neighbourhood as the object of assessment and b) how tools and systems for planning, managing and assessing the sustainability of neighbourhood design (in the absolute sense of a performance measurement) and the sustainable development of existing neighbourhoods (in terms of process-related support by target systems and performance monitoring) respond to these tasks and features.

## 1.1 New and Existing Neighbourhoods as the Object of Assessment – Barriers

The neighbourhood represents a meso-level of analysis and action between the city (and its parts) and individual structures, buildings, or groups of buildings. Unlike cities and individual buildings, neighbourhoods display no clear references to institutional and administrative boundaries. This complicates the definition and demarcation of neighbourhoods which can be made from a spatial, social, administrative, or contextual perspective. Spatial system boundaries are adjusted to fit the characteristics of specific criteria (including energy supply, trade, mobility, identity/sense of community). Very heterogeneous groups of actors are involved in neighbourhood development, some of which operate in informal (e.g. Local Agenda 21) or formal (e.g. property owners' associations) networks. Neighbourhoods exhibit no static state, but instead are always in permanent development. Thus, it is very difficult to describe a functional equivalent for constituting a basis for the comparison of different neighbourhood types and assessment results. On the one hand, the "function" of a neighbourhood can hardly be defined and, on the other hand, there are neighbourhoods with different characteristics (residential, mixed use, industrial area, etc.). Appropriate systems for planning, managing or assessing the sustainability of neighbourhoods or of their development must respond to these characteristics.

## 1.2 Existing Solutions and Experiences in Germany

Germany has a long tradition in the field of development and application of tools for assessing sustainable urban and neighbourhood development. Among other approaches, indicator sets and systems have been developed (cf. Fuhrich 2001, pp. 13f.; Liepach et al. 2003; Spreter et al. 2004). These are used to describe goals and monitor performances and sometimes to support decisions within the framework of Local Agenda 21. Sustainable urban and neighbourhood development is a process that must be actively monitored and supported.

Requirements for sustainable urban development, which include mostly development at the city level, are part of the National Sustainable Development Strategy in Germany initiated by the Federal Government in 2002 and followed by progress reports. Here, a focus on land use is emphasized. Comprehensive requirements are also formulated in the German Building Code (BauGB 2004). Therein, the task of urban development planning is described as follows: "The development plans shall ensure a sustainable urban development, which reconciles social, economic and environmental protection requirements with the responsibility towards future generations, and is socially fair and in the service of bettering public land use. They should help to ensure a more humane environment, to protect and develop natural resources and to promote, particularly in urban development, climate change mitigation and adaptation, as well as to preserve and architecturally develop the urban form as well as that of the town and landscape" (BauGB 2014, Part 1, § 1; (5)). Based on the goals and tasks described here, requirements and indicators can be formulated and developed.

The German Sustainable Building Council (DGNB) has developed and introduced a certification system for describing and assessing the sustainability of new neighbourhood developments (cf. DGNB 2012). It follows the basic structure of certification systems for buildings. What is really assessed is the result of the planning and implementation of a new neighbourhood, and thus the level of performance achieved at a defined point in time.

At present, an intensive discussion is taking place in Germany in relation to the assessment of the sustainability of neighbourhoods (in universities the theme of sustainable campus development is also being discussed). Specifically, this discussion deals with questions such as:

- How can the object of an assessment (a given neighbourhood) be defined, circumscribed and made comparable to others?
- What are the differences between the approach of "target definition and performance monitoring" on the one hand, and the approach of "performance measurement" on the other?
- Is there a risk of stigmatising neighbourhoods with poor quality based on the results of an assessment following the "performance measurement" approach?
- Can approaches such as "target definition and performance monitoring" support the process of sustainable neighbourhood development and have an influence on how key players are identified and involved in the process?
- Can the "target definition and performance monitoring" approach be harmonised with the "performance measurement" approach (e.g. by using similar criteria and indicators)?
- Can the tools for describing, assessing and monitoring sustainable neighbourhood development be combined with models for mobilizing landowners (e.g. housing improvement districts – HID [cf. Krueger et al. 2007])?

These issues were addressed by the authors in a Karlsruhe Institute of Technology (KIT) internal research project (cf. Balouktsi/Luetzkendorf 2013). As a first step, an analysis of existing international and national approaches and methods has been developed. In this paper, selected results and findings are presented and discussed.

# 2 The Overall Context

Within the spectrum of global, national and local approaches, cities play a crucial role to globally advance sustainable development given their share of global population, global GDP, resource use, $CO_2$ emissions, and associated dynamics (cf. Wheeler/Beatley 2009). They are complex systems, particularly in the cases of global megacities, which at the same time cause and are affected by global change phenomena such as climate change. Being engines of societal development, melting pots of different cultures, and places of high accumulation of capital, knowledge and human resources, innovation potential, etc., they offer great opportunities to deal with these challenges and to make strides towards sustainable development.

Governance for sustainable urban development requires both a suitable conceptual basis and analytical tools to define criteria as a basic goal or direction for development, to assess state and development performances, and to design and assess measures to improve performances. Mainly due to the variety of existing local conditions and interests of involved actors, a general and standardized definition of sustainable urban development does not exist to date. While in developing countries, priorities are definitely set on existing problems and their solutions, urban strategies in industrialized countries are more focused on environmental and health problems, urban sprawl, climate protection or urban quality of life in general (cf. Clark 2010; Jenks/Jones 2010). “Compact Cities”, “Resilient Cities”, “Smart Cities” or “EcoCities” are dominating catchwords and initiatives here.

Nevertheless, integrated or integrative approaches are often and increasingly demanded in this context across countries, but still rarely implemented in practice. “Integrative” is understood here particularly with respect to thematic issues of development, scientific disciplines, sectors, scales, and actors. Thematic integration is the basic idea of the Integrative Sustainability concept of the German Helmholtz Association focusing on the postulate of inter- and intra-generational justice, and its substantiation for the general goals of securing human existence, maintaining society’s productive potential and preserving society’s options for development and action (cf. Kopfmueller et al. 2001). It is one of the very few scientific concepts that is applied systematically in a range of project and consultancy activities in Germany, Europe and outside Europe (cf. Grunwald/Kopfmueller 2012; cf. Kopfmueller 2006) and provides the conceptual background for this paper as well.

Regarding the aspect of varying scales, three main perspectives have to be considered in research, assessment, planning and governance of urban systems: the total city (including city-rural interrelations), neighbourhoods, and single buildings (associated more directly with subjects such as construction materials, technologies, etc.). Each of these scales displays its own characteristics and contributions to support or constrain sustainable development and should thus be addressed separately as well as considering the relevant interrelations with other scales to meet the requirements of integration. Besides the respective characteristics and properties of the levels of analysis, which can be expressed in the form of a specific functional equivalent, there is important information (e.g. energy and material flows) that is passed from the lower to upper levels.

While the city and the building levels have conceptually and analytically been addressed for many years, neighbourhoods are increasingly shifting their focus to research and policy (cf. Wiliams et al. 2010). Buildings originally marked the starting point for sustainability assessments in the context of human settlements. In addition to buildings, the interactions of residents and in turn their interaction with the environment influence emissions and resource consumption levels, and this need to expand the scope to other scales leads to a stronger focus on neighbourhoods.

This intermediate scale is considered as an archetype of human communities. It brings science and planning closer to the needs and real-life circumstances of people, where strong interrelationships to support sustainable development can be created and maintained. At the city level, particularly in big cities, human settlements and interactions are considered foremostly as functional units, while at the neighbourhood level, community, identity and solidarity aspects are more relevant and can be found (or at least be initiated) more often. At this level, human needs and demands (such as mobility, basic supply of water, energy etc.) can be better examined than at the building level, and the neighbourhood size is more manageable analytically and politically compared with the city level. In addition, the various characteristics of a city (densities, cultural diversities, etc.) and their diversities can be considered here much more thoroughly than at the larger city scale, and interactions between different economic, physical and social sub-systems can be analysed more adequately.

Neighbourhoods play an integral role in forming community and social networks. Within the boundaries of neighbourhoods, more opportunities exist for social and political expression and participation. The level of involvement, engagement and motivation of different actors to participate in decisions influencing their living environment and conditions is higher compared with the city level because residents are involved here more directly and share relatively more homogenous living experiences (cf. Wilson 2009, pp. 1f.). In light of this, interventions at a neighbourhood level provide alternative and often more promising options for a transition to sustainability.

This approach could be an important contribution to an integrated sustainable urban planning and development process, focusing on elements such as overcoming sectorally fragmented planning and policy strategies, longer-term perspectives beyond usual election periods, and close involvement of civil society stakeholders in decision processes. This in turn could be part of what could be called a "culture of sustainable development" (cf. Parodi 2011), including changes in culture (lifestyles), policy (sectoral coherence and integration, long-terms views, etc.), institutions, and conditions to set appropriate incentives for these changes in the political and institutional framework.

# 3 Review of Sustainability Assessment Systems

## 3.1 Certification Systems and Decision Support Tools – an Overview

The increasing acknowledgement and understanding that the path to sustainability passes through the broader context of the urban environment led to the recent development of several international (and national) sustainability assessment systems on the neighbourhood level (also sometimes referred to as "districts" or "communities"). These can be divided into two main categories, the first includes the systems that emerged from existing and established third-party assessment and certification systems for buildings (such as LEED, BREEAM, CASBEE, DGNB etc.). The second category includes the systems embedded into neighbourhood-scale plans and sustainability initiatives intended mostly to be used as planning and decision-making support tools (first-party and second-party assessment systems) (cf. Sharifi/Murayama 2013). In this paper, wherever the term "systems" is used, it refers to the first category, and wherever the term "tools" is used, reference is made to the second category. An overview of the most well-known systems and tools at a neighbourhood scale is given in Table 1.

In this paper, both a well-founded survey of the characteristics of existing systems and tools, and a method for comparing them at different scales will be presented. More than ten international tools specific to addressing sustainability at a neighbourhood scale were chosen as a reference in an internal KIT study performed by the authors based on the accessibility and completeness of available information, the coverage level of sustainability, the representation of different parts of the world and the scoring process. The analysed systems and tools include LEED for Neighborhood Development (LEED-ND), BREEAM for Communities (BfC), CASBEE for Urban Development (CASBEE-UD), Estidama Pearl Community Rating System (PCRS), QSAS for Neighborhoods (QSAS-NH), Green Star Communities (GSC), Earthcraft Communities (ECC), DGNB Neubau Stadtquartier (DGNB-NSQ) Sustainable Community Rating (SCR) and the EU projects HQE2R and Ecocity.

Table 1: Some of the Most Well-known Systems and Tools

| | *System/Tool's Name* | *Developer(s)* | *Region* | *Version** |
|---|---|---|---|---|
| *Systems* | LEED-ND | USGBC, CNU, and NRDC | US | 2009 (2007) |
| | ECC | Greater Atlanta HBA & others | US | 2003 |
| | BREEAM Communities | BRE | UK | 2009 |
| | CASBEE-UD | JSBC and JaGBC | Japan | 2007 (2006) |
| | ESTIDAMA Pearls | Abu Dhabi UPC | Abu Dhabi | 2010 |
| | QSAS Neighborhoods | GORD | Qatar | 2011 |
| | Green Star Communities | GBCA | Australia | 2012 |
| | Green Mark for Districts | BCA | Singapore | 2009 |
| | GPR-Stedenbouw<br>DGNB-NSQ | City of Groningen & others<br>DGNB | Denmark<br>Germany | 2011<br>2012 (2011) |
| *Tools* | HQE$^2$R | CSTB | EU | 2001–2004 |
| | Ecocity | EU research project | EU | 2002–2005 |
| | SCR | Victorian State Government | Australia | 2007 |
| | EcoDistricts | POSI | US | 2010 |
| | SPeAR | ARUP | UK | 2011 (2000) |
| | SuBET | HILSON MORAN & others | UK | 2008–2010 |
| | One Planet Living (OPL) | BioRegional Development Group and WWF International | UK | 2008 |
| | SMEO-Quartiere | BFE and ARE | Switzerland | 2011 |
| | Beacon Neighbourhood Sustainability Framework | Beacon | New Zealand | 2010 |
| | Cascadia Scorecard | Sightline Institute | US | 2004 |

* The date inside the parenthesis indicates the first version of the tool.

Authors' Archive

## 3.2 Methodology for the Comparative Analysis

Tools and systems to support the planning, monitoring and assessment of the sustainability of neighbourhoods have already been compared (cf. Haapio 2012). In some cases these comparisons differ in terms of scope and depth of analysis. For the comparison of tools and systems for the present paper, a generalised approach has been developed and applied which is briefly discussed below. General characteristics are described and an analysis at different levels is carried out. The following issues are examined:

(a) object of assessment (existing neighbourhood, new neighbourhood development, etc.);
(b) basic character (planning support system, certification system with absolute assessment of sustainability, target value system to support sustainable neighbourhood development, etc.);
(c) included dimensions of sustainability – Level 1 (economic, environmental and/or social dimension, possibly supplemented by an institutional dimension);
(d) the assessment criteria included in each dimension – Level 2;
(e) included indicators in each criterion – Level 3.

In this paper, the topics (a) and (b) are addressed in detail and examples are given for the 3 levels of analysis (c) to (e).

## 3.3 Results of the Comparative Analysis of the Selected Tools and Systems

As a first step, the selected tools and systems are compared across the criteria (a) and (b), as discussed above, to provide both an example of such an analysis and an overview of the existing situation. The results are presented in Table 2.

Table 2: Comparative Analysis of the Selected Systems and Tools

| | *Systems* | | | | | | | | *Tools* | | |
|---|---|---|---|---|---|---|---|---|---|---|---|
| *Criteria* | LEED ND | BfC | CASBEE UD | PCRS | QSAS-NH | GSC | DGNB NSQ | ECC | HQE2R | Ecocity | SCR |
| *Object of Assessment* | | | | | | | | | | | |
| New neighbourhood developments | X | X | X | X | X | X | X | X | | X | X |
| Existing neighbourhoods as an object | | | X | | X | | | | X | X | X |
| Existing neighbourhoods as a process | | | | | | | | | X | | |
| *Character* | | | | | | | | | | | |
| Performance oriented assessment | X | X | X | X | X | X | X | X | X | X | X |
| Target distance & performance monitoring | | | | | | | | | X | | |

X indicates that these criteria are addressed to a satisfactory degree.

Authors' Archive

Subsequently, examples of the comparison at different levels are provided (criteria (c) to (e)), in order to show how the relative value of each tool and system in covering all the important issues related to sustainable development should be investigated. Examples are presented in Tables 3, 4 and 5.

Table 3: Level of Inclusion of the Dimensions of Sustainability – Level 1

| | *Systems* | | | | | | | | *Tools* | | |
|---|---|---|---|---|---|---|---|---|---|---|---|
| *Criteria* | LEED ND | BfC | CASBEE UD | PCRS | QSAS-NH | GSC | DGNB NSQ | ECC | HQE2R | Ecocity | SCR |
| *Sustainability Coverage* | | | | | | | | | | | |
| Environmental | X | X | X | X | X | X | X | X | X | X | X |
| Social | X | X | X | X | X | X | X | X | X | X | X |
| Economic | | X | | | | X | X | | X | X | X |
| Institutional | | X | | X | | X | X | X | X | X | X |

Authors' Archive

When dealing with each tool's object of assessment, it is important to clarify whether these can be applied to existing neighbourhoods. This is a major challenge, given that the worldwide percentage of existing neighbourhoods exceeds by far the percentage and rate of increase of newly developed ones. But when assessing the existing neighbourhood (as an object), there is the danger of stigmatizing a neighbourhood as "unsustainable", based only on its performance at a specific point of time, potentially discouraging planners and developers from working in such neighbourhoods. In reality, an existing neighbourhood and its development is not an object but a process, as it changes and evolves continuously through time. Therefore, the authors suggest that when dealing with existing neighbourhoods it is more appropriate to assess their progression (positive or negative development) over time instead of their performance at a iven time for supporting the decision making process.

A system or tool of measurement typically determines whether a development is sustainable or whether progress is being made towards sustainability (cf. Reed et al. 2009). The character of the assessment system or tool significantly influences its ability to function as a decision support system. Most of the existing sustainability assessment systems are performance oriented, where credit points are awarded based on the level of performance in various areas to specify whether a neighbourhood is sustainable or not. Therefore, particular attention should be paid to the ability of some systems and tools to track temporal changes in the sustainability of existing neighbourhoods or renovation projects and to specify whether they are moving in the right direction towards achieving specific short-term or longer-term sustainable develop-

Table 4: Level of Inclusion of Economic and Institutional Sustainability Criteria – Level 2

| | *Systems* | | | | | | | | *Tools* | | |
|---|---|---|---|---|---|---|---|---|---|---|---|
| *Criteria* | LEED ND | BfC | CASBEE UD | PCRS | QSAS-NH | GSC | DGNB NSQ | ECC | HQE2R | Ecocity | SCR |
| *Economic Sustainability* | | | | | | | | | | | |
| Skill education and employment | X | X | | | | X | | X | X | X | X |
| Community investment | | X | | | | X | | | | X | X |
| Value stability | | | | | | | X | | | | |
| Space efficiency | | | | | | | X | | | | |
| Support of national economy | | | | | X | | | | | | |
| Residential incentives | | | | | | X | | | | | |
| Housing affordability | X | X | | | | X | | X | X | | X |
| Costs and benefits assessment | | | | X | | X | X | | | X | X |
| Fiscal impact on the community | | | | | | | X | | | | |
| *Institutional Sustainability* | | | | | | | | | | | |
| Active participation in decisions | X | X | X | | | X | X | X | X | X | X |
| Integrated development strategy | | X | | X | | X | X | | | X | X |
| Strong voluntary sector | | X | | | | | X | X | X | | |
| Engagement in the SD process | | | | X | | X | X | X | X | | |
| Community management | X | X | | | | X | X | X | | | X |
| Environmental management | | | X | X | X | X | X | | | | |
| Adaptation and resilience | | X | | | | X | | | | | |
| Quality assurance and monitoring | | | | | | | X | | | | |

Table 5: Level of Inclusion of Different Indicators under a Specific Criterion – Level 3

| *Cost and Benefit Assessments* | *PCRS* | *GSC* | *DGNB NSQ* | *Ecocity* | *SCR* |
|---|---|---|---|---|---|
| Life cycle costing (LCC) | X | | X | | |
| Return on investment (ROI) | | X | | | |
| Cost/return ratio | | | | X | |
| Internal rate of return (IRR) | | | | | X |
| Gross margins | | | | | X |

Authors' Archive

ment targets (distance-to-target approach). This type of assessment can be of high relevance, especially for achieving the vision of continuous improvement. Engagement with the concept of continuous improvement in sustainability through effective monitoring and feedback at all levels is already a trend in the context of existing buildings (sustainability assessment for buildings in-use) and this should also be integrated into the assessment of sustainable development of existing neighbourhoods (cf. Egan 2004, pp. 20f.).

As discussed before, the idea of measuring the relative success of a neighbourhood (instead of the absolute) by comparing performance levels at different points in time or time periods has been discussed in Germany since 2004 (cf. Fuhrich 2004, p. 9). However, this idea arose too soon to influence different actors in this direction. From another point of view, already existing systems that assessed sustainable buildings were adapted to the neighbourhood scale, where in most cases the neighbourhood (existing or new) is assessed as an object and not as a process. However, it should be noted that this method of assessment is suitable only for dealing with new neighbourhood developments and not with existing ones. The negative result of such an assessment is the potential cost of decreasing property values and leaving a stigma on an existing neighbourhood, making it difficult to maintain the community's ambition to implement changes.

Among the analyzed systems and tools, HQE2R is the only one that addresses temporal changes of performance assessment and allows the decision makers to evaluate if their actions help to achieve the targets they set. To follow this good example of the application of the "target distance and performance monitoring" approach, the other systems and tools should inform and adjust their methodology.

The competence of different systems and tools in measuring sustainable development, in other words their degree of sustainability criteria coverage, has always been a major issue to be investigated. It should be noted that in recent years the framework of assessment has been expanded from merely covering environmental impacts to achieving a balance between environmental, social, and economic performance. As a further step, the importance of institutional sustainability as the fourth pillar has also been emphasized (cf. Parris/Kates 2003). This pillar complements the others by considering the participation of all community stakeholders in the decision making process, as well as the community management and governance mechanisms. In this context, some new certification systems and some currently under development (e.g. the new version of BfG and the recently developed GSC) have already considered the inclusion of governance as a main category. This should also be taken into account when refining existing tools.

Although the goal of achieving sustainability is common within sustainable neighbourhood assessment systems and tools, this is pursued in different ways. Despite the structural similarities of these tools and systems, the included categories, criteria, and indicators are not the same in every case. This makes comparisons more complicated, especially at higher levels. A comparison among the tools and systems can be performed at different levels, as for example at an indicator, criteria or main category (or sustainability dimension) level. A comparison at the highest level (sustainability dimensions) has been provided in Table 3. An example of a comparative analysis at a meso-level is presented in Table 4, where important criteria were gathered from the selected systems and tools to indicate the coverage of specific sustainability criteria under the economic and institutional dimension. However, it is always more accurate to compare at an indicator level, as similar criteria can be assessed by different indicators. This is clearly illustrated in Table 5, where an indicator level comparison under the economic criterion "cost and benefit assessment" is presented as an example to highlight the different possibilities available, just to assess a single criterion.

It is clear that at the level of indicators and sub-indicators, there are substantial differences among the systems. It is therefore recommended that in addition to the reporting and documentation of complex assessment results, a detailed breakdown of the individual results indicating all criteria and weighting factors should also always be published and expected by the different stakeholders. This is a prerequisite for ensuring transparency.

The assessment of the sustainability of communities and a sustainable community development is currently the subject of international standardization. Specifically, in 2012 ISO created the ISO/TC 268 Committee on "sustainable development in communities". This Committee is responsible for three standards: the ISO/CD 37101 "Sustainable development and resilience of communities – Management systems – General principles and requirements" (under development), the ISO 37120:2014 "Sustainable development of communities – Indicators for city services and quality of life" (published) and the ISO/AWI TR 37121 "Inventory and review of existing indicators on sustainable development and resilience in cities" (under development).

## 3.4 Recommendations

As a result of the analysis, it can be stated that in the current international and national context there is an increasing focus on the assessment and certification of new settlements and neighbourhoods. The various systems applied usually derive from the tradition of sustainability certification of buildings. They differ greatly in many aspects and need to be analyzed in great detail in order to determine the comparability of their outcomes. These certification systems are a useful tool for the planning and implementation of new settlements and neighbourhoods, and in particular can motivate developers to think more towards sustainable solutions.

Of course, this does not solve the problem of the (further) development and sustainability-related improvement of existing neighbourhoods, especially of those with several owners of land and buildings. Here, it is recommended to proceed with the traditions of the Local Agenda 21. Tools are needed that will specifically help to design tailored concepts and goals to concrete situations, provide a method of monitoring the implementation, and measuring success in reaching these goals. Thus, neighbourhoods with a poorer initial performance have a chance to be improved in this respect. One basic advantage of this particular approach lies in its participatory model, as local actors are involved in the design of policies and objectives.

Therefore, the authors recommend that such an approach should be pushed and supported even more than has been done so far. There are already existing examples aiming at the energy-related improvement of neighbourhoods. In the context of the funding programme of the German state-owned KfW Bank, there are models to provide financial support to the “rehabilitation managers” at the neighbourhood level, who can act as coordinators (cf. KfW 2011). It is recommended that this approach be extended to sustainable neighbourhood development, and to consider the energy-related component as a sub-theme. Conceptually, this approach can be applied by community/property owners associations (cf. Baba et al. 2011).

The existing assessment tools and systems analysed in this paper clearly mark progress in expanding from the building to the neighbourhood level and the scope of applied assessment criteria. However, there are still gaps and deficiencies remaining, particularly with respect to building an integrative understanding as outlined above, and in the development of more detailed policy and planning procedures.

With respect to possible future activities, the authors would propose a two-step procedure: first, a modular kit could be provided to potential users. This kit should allow for better distinguishing between newly constructed and already existing neighbourhoods, and include an expanded sustainability criteria set which better considers, for instance, cultural aspects, alternative economic aspects (such as discounting practices in investment decisions) or social coherence aspects. Such a kit could be used as a basis for particular assessment contexts. Two elements are to be emphasized here: the design and implementation of the kit has to involve relevant local stakeholders, and should fulfil certain thematic and procedural minimum requirements. Secondly, this kit could be the basis for discussions about possibilities and limits of certain standardizations of assessment processes on neighbourhood levels, and of political commitment to results for involved actors.

At Karlsruhe Institute of Technology (KIT), the findings outlined in this paper will be used and further developed in the context of the cooperation with the City of Karlsruhe (Project "Real-Labor") and in relation to the idea of sustainable campus development.

# 4 Integration into Overall Concepts and Developments

Sustainability assessment is not an end in itself. Its purpose is to support sustainable urban and neighbourhood development. This is influenced and driven by various actors. Many actors are involved, especially during the process of developing an existing neighbourhood , in contrast to the planning of new neighbourhoods through a developer. More than ever in Germany and elsewhere, there is a growing political commitment towards the inclusion of these actors and the mobilization of their capital for a strengthening of the neighbourhoods. One approach, among others, is the model of Housing Improvement Districts (HID) (cf. Krueger et al. 2007). These initiatives require organizational and contextual support. A useful addition to the involvement of planners and facilitators are tools for the formulation of common goals, as well as to verify the achievement of objectives (success). Suitable for this purpose, inter alia, are the sustainability rating systems. The focus of their application does not lie in a certification but in their ability to function as a checklist, a useful tool for monitoring and documentation.

One can arrive at very similar conclusions when considering the introduction of sustainable property funds (cf. Buegl et al. 2009). Part of this is oriented toward the improvement of neighbourhoods. In this case, effective means and instruments are also required for presenting and communicating the initial state and the improvement or "level of sustainability" attained.

Sustainability assessment is no longer seen only in connection with issues such as reputation, image or marketing. A change is clearly apparent. Sustainability assessment systems are increasingly becoming a useful and valuable tool for planners, investors and citizens – these efforts must be continued.

## Acknowledgements

The authors would like to thank the KIT for supporting this research project with funding from the start-up program.

## References

Baba, L.; Fryczewski, I.; Wilbert, K.; Metzmacher, M.; Tantow, D. (2011): Leitfaden Eigentümerstandortgemeinschaften. Empfehlungen zur Gründung und Begleitung von Eigentümerstandortgemeinschaften. Berlin (BMVBS) (in German)

Balouktsi, M.; Luetzkendorf, T. (2013): Critical Analysis of Sustainable Neighbourhood Assessment Systems. Karlsruhe

BauGB – Baugesetzbuch. 1960/2014. – URL: http://www.gesetze-im-internet.de/bundesrecht/bbaug/gesamt.pdf (in German)

Buegl, R.; Leimgruber, C.; Hueni, G. R.; Scholz, R. W. (2009): Sustainable Property Funds. Financial Stakeholders' Views on Sustainability Criteria and Market Acceptance. In: Building Research & Information, Vol. 37, No. 3, pp. 246–63

Clark, W. (2008): Sustainable Communities Design Handbook. Green Engineering, Architecture, and Technology. Oxford

DGNB – Deutsche Gesellschaft für Nachhaltiges Bauen e.V. (2012): Neubau Stadtquartiere: DGNB Handbuch für nachhaltiges Bauen. Stuttgart (in German)

Ebert, T.; Eßig, N.; Hauser, G. (2011): Green Building Certification Systems. Institut für internationale Architekturdokumentation. Munich (Institut für internationale Architekturdokumentation)

Egan, S. J. (2004): The Egan Review: Skills for Sustainable Communities. London (Office of the Deputy Prime Minister)

FGG – Federal Government of Germany (2002): Perspectives for Germany: Our Strategy for Sustainable Development. Berlin

Fuhrich, M. (2001): Kompass für den Weg zur Stadt der Zukunft. Indikatorengestützte Erfolgskontrolle nachhaltiger Stadtentwicklung. Eine Orientierungshilfe. Bonn (in German)

Fuhrich, M. (2004): Städte der Zukunft: Kompass für den Weg zur Stadt der Zukunft. Bonn (in German)

Grunwald, A.; Kopfmueller J. (2012): Nachhaltigkeit. Eine Einführung. Frankfurt am Main/New York (in German)

Haapio, A. (2012): Towards Sustainable Urban Communities. In: Environmental Impact Assessment Review, Vol. 32, pp. 165–169

Jenks, M.; Jones, C. (eds.) (2010): Dimensions of the Sustainable City. Dortrecht a.o.

Keating, M. (1993): Agenda for Change: A Plain Language Version of Agenda 21 and Other Rio Agreements. Geneva (Centre for Our Common Future)

KfW-Bankengruppe (2011): Energetische Stadtsanierung – Zuschüsse für integrierte Quartierskonzepte und Sanierungsmanager (432). – URL: https://www.kfw.de/KfW-Konzern/Service/Download-Center/F%C3%B6rderprogramme-%28Inlandsf.%29-%28D-EN%29/Barrierefreie-Dokumente/Energetische-Stadtsanierung-Zusch%C3%BCsse-f%C3%BCr-Quartierskonzepte-%28432%29-Merkblatt/

Kopfmueller, J.; Brandl, V.; Joerissen J.; Paetau, M.; Banse, G.; Coenen, R.; Grunwald, A. (2001): Nachhaltige Entwicklung integrativ betrachtet. Konstitutive Elemente, Regeln, Indikatoren. Berlin (in German)

Kopfmueller, J. (2006): Ein Konzept auf dem Prüfstand. Das integrative Nachhaltigkeitskonzept in der Forschungspraxis. Berlin (in German)

Krueger, T.; Wickel, M.; Kreuz, S. (2007): Gutachten über die Begleitforschung für das Teilprojekt HID Steilshoop im Rahmen des Projektes Lebenswerte Stadt Hamburg. Hamburg (HafenCity Universität) (in German)

Liepach, K.; Sixt, J.; Irrek, W. (2003): Kommunale Nachhaltigkeitsindikatoren: Vom Datenfriedhof zur zentralen Steuerungsinformation – Municipal Sustainability Indicators: From the Data Graveyard to Central Control Information. Wuppertal (Wuppertal Institut für Klima, Umwelt, Energie) (Wuppertal Papers, No 138)

Parodi, O. (2011): Three Steps towards a Culture of Sustainability. In: Parodi O.; Ayestaran, I.; Banse, G. (eds.): Sustainable Development – Relationships to Culture, Knowledge and Ethics. Karlsruhe, pp. 75–92

Parris, T. M.; Kates, R. W. (2003): Characterizing and Measuring Sustainable Development. In: Annual Review of Environment and Resources, Vol. 28, pp 559–586

Reed, R.; Bilos, A.; Wilkinson, S.; Schulte, K. W. (2009): International Comparison of Sustainable Rating Tools. In: Journal of Sustainable Real Estate, Vol. 1, No. 1, pp. 1–22

Sharifi, A.; Murayama, A. (2013): A Critical Review of Seven Selected Neighborhood Sustainability Assessment Tools. In: Environmental Impact Assessment Review, Vol. 8, pp. 73–87

Spreter, R.; Vollmer, C.; Neitzke, H. P.; Korczak, D.; Hoffmann, A (2004): Indikatoren-Set: Zukunftsfähige Kommune. Radolfzell (Deutsche Umwelthilfe) (in German)

Wheeler, S.; Beatley, T. (eds.) (2009): The Sustainable Urban Development Reader (2nd ed.). London

Wiliams, K.; Dair, C.; Lindsay, M. (2010): Neighbourhood Design and Sustainable Lifestyles. In: Jenks, M.; Jones, C. (eds.): Dimensions of the Sustainable City. Dordrecht, pp. 183–214

Wilson, R. E. (2009): Why Neighborhoods Matter. The Importance of Geographic Composition. In: A Quarterly Bulletin of Applied Geography for the Study of Crime & Public Safety, Vol. 2, No. 2, pp. 1–2

# 2. Research and Development Processes

katja saar

# "District Future – Urban Lab"

## A Real Urban Transition Lab

*Oliver Parodi, Marius Albiez, Sarah Meyer-Soylu, Colette Waitz*

## 1 An Initial Overview

The sustainable development of our cities is one of the most demanding challenges of the 21st century. The Urban Transition Lab "*District Future – Urban Lab*",[1] an urban research and development project in and for Karlsruhe, provides the conceptual framework for joint experiments and research on potentially sustainable societal and technological innovations originating from the urban society and the Karlsruhe Institute of Technology (KIT) (cf. Parodi 2011; Parodi et al. 2015).

Guided by the integrative concept of sustainable development (cf. Kopfmüller et al. 2001), the project works transdisciplinarily towards the mutual stimulation and co-operation of science, politics, citizenry, and the private sector. Always focusing on the global context, this alliance tries out sustainable solutions which shall provide a long-term role model for other, especially European, cities in terms of their quality, number, and concentration. The main objective of this project, which is participatory in nature, is the gradual transformation of Karlsruhe's Oststadt into a sustainable urban district. In the end, it is about a dense sustainability and about entrenching an actively supported culture of sustainability (cf. Parodi 2010, 2015; Parodi et al. 2011) in the urban space. Other important characteristics of the project are:

- Sustainable development of the existing district;
- creating and researching a *compact sustainability* and exploring interdependencies, synergies, and conflicting goals;
- scientific public-private partnerships and providing benefits of KIT to the city and region of Karlsruhe
- establishment of the overall concept of sustainability in urban life; education for sustainable development and the development of new qualities of life;
- transdisciplinary generation of system, orientation, and transformation knowledge.

---

1 Cf. www.quartierzukunft.de. In the following, the short form "District Future" is used as a synonym for the project.

The Urban Transition Lab *District Future* is designed as a creative platform that provides a framework for numerous concrete projects ("real experiments") of sustainable urban development. Its multidisciplinary team will continue to develop the urban transition lab over the next years without predetermined outcomes, research and network, co-ordinate and chair project activities in the fields of mobility, housing, social participation, energy, economy, health, culture, work and leisure, education, environmental protection, and life satisfaction.

*District Future* was initiated in 2012, is led by the Institute for Technology Assessment and Systems Analysis of KIT and is realized in co-operation with numerous actors in Karlsruhe and at the KIT.[2]

# 2 The Context: Cities as Necessary Places of Sustainable Development

For the first time in human history, more people are living in cities than in rural areas – and this share will continue to rise (cf. UN 2014b, p. 7). The share of people living in cities in Asia, Latin America, but also increasingly in the African region, has grown by approximately 30 percent (cf. UN 2014b, p. 8) since the 1950 (compared to the total population). This is also reflected by the large number of metropolises which have emerged over the last 30 years (cf. UN 2014a), especially in China and India. While the urbanization level in these regions increases due to new buildings, a trend towards reurbanization and redensification of existing urban spaces can be observed in Europe (cf. Brake 2011).

Also central-European cities are confronted with growing challenges: The negative impacts of climate change, demographic change, especially an increasingly aging society, social inequality, and the damage to the environment are some of the challenges that cities have to face today and in the future. In addition, consumer goods and energy have to be imported from the surroundings and from all over the world to satisfy the needs of the urban population. This, in turn, results in huge amounts and a high concentration of waste and emissions (cf. Ackermann 2005). Thus cities themselves become multipliers of crisis and produce effects that go far beyond their city boundaries. Therefore the sustainable development of urban spaces, which implies the concurrent improvement of their resilience, is one of the most urgent challenges of our time.

Today's problems and future challenges must not be considered separately in this context since they are always part of larger and complex interrelations in the context of socio-technology, the natural environment, and economics (cf., e.g., WBGU 1996). Demographic change in central-European cities is one of the reasons for the growing

2 Cf. http://www.itas.kit.edu/num_lp_paro11_quazu.php & www.quartierzukunft.de.

demand for barrier-free housing. However, in particular elderly people who are no longer working and only have a low income are often affected by displacement processes (cf. Aehnelt et al. 2009). This is aggravated by the fact that especially elderly people have to suffer from negative aspects of climate change, for example from heat waves during the summer months (cf. Matzarakis 2013). Nevertheless, based on their socio-technical complexity, cities also provide a suitable framework for experiments which will finally – at least potentially – advance systems innovations and a sustainable development (cf. Schneidewind 2014; Schneidewind/Scheck 2013). In addition, cities meet a multitude of needs, combine diversity in a small area (cf. Schneidewind 2014; Schneidewind/Scheck 2013) and thus provide the precondition for social and technological innovations. The urban transition lab *District Future* wants to update these potentials to transform an existing ward of the city of Karlsruhe into a sustainable one.

## 3 District Future – Urban Lab: Main Characteristics

Due to its research nature, the research methods applied, and the transformative purpose, the project sees itself as an urban transition lab and meets the necessary framework conditions (cf. MWK 2013; Schneidewind 2014; Schneidewind/Scheck 2013): Sustainable development is elaborated and implemented in co-design in a transdisciplinary process set for the long term. The researchers of *District Future* with their dual role also consider themselves as explicit and declared drivers for sustainable development. Depending on the current subject, other relevant disciplines at KIT are involved in the activities of the urban transition lab as well. Level of action is that of the district, the mezzanine between building and city which provides an urban and almost complete microcosm with all its areas of need and life; at the same time the project area remains "manageable for the research process" (Schneidewind 2014, p. 4) without losing the socio-technical complexity that is important for sustainable systems innovations. In addition, we can find specifics (cf. Tiddens 2014) at the district level – e.g. in governance, social vicinity, and regarding the residents' identification with their "quarter" – which are fascinating for the realization of sustainable development, but have not received much attention to date.

The crucial factor for the success of a *dense sustainable development* is the (collective, if possible) commitment of a preferably large and diverse group of actors of the urban society, especially of its citizens. Therefore *District Future* is a platform for co-design in the first place and wants to involve actors of the urban society actively and directly in the research and development process (Citizen Science approach). A comprehensive and integrative sustainable urban development can only succeed if a large number of people contribute to it. Thus *District Future* thrives on participation, pursues urban development in a collective approach.

Figure 1: With a "Mach mit!" (Join us!) letter all (approx. 7.000) households in the project area were informed of the *District Future* in 2013 and invited to actively join the project

Source: District Future

The project takes sustainable development, an overall concept developed by the United Nations, seriously and wants to assess ecological, social, economic, cultural, and institutional matters in Karlsruhe in an integrative way and bring it to life in a scientifically sound way. The co-operation between urban society and KIT provides an experimental space to test new forward-looking ideas, societal and technological innovations, and life plans. Therefore not only suggestions for sustainable urban development provided by the urban society are seized in practice, but also KIT inventions are tested and researched within the urban space. They will then be further developed, projected, evaluated, and, at best, established, involving scientific findings and competencies.

# 4 Project Objectives

The main objective of the project is to transform the Oststadt, an existing urban district in Karlsruhe, in a long-term, dialogue-based process into a sustainable neighbourhood. This is based on a comprehensive and integrative understanding of sustainability which focuses its action on a global, intergenerational justice (cf. Kopfmüller et al.

2001; Seebacher et al. 2014).[3] According to these values, we aim at an urban development which overcomes sectoral needs and individual interests within the city and also considers references, effects, and internal and external responsibilities of urban actors at both the regional and the global level (e.g. via commodity or cash flows).

Another aim is the development of what already exists. The future challenges of sustainable urban development are the sustainable reshaping of our existing cities, not extensive new constructions. The city of the future is – at least in Europe and North America – already built. It is not about founding new cities, but dealing with the existing ones in a future-oriented approach. Therefore the task is to develop the existing, i.e. use the status quo of the urban structure, and provide a forward-looking perspective for a sustainable urban development. The approach and concept of *District Future* shall serve as a model here and be transferable to other (especially European) cities. This transferability is possible through the use of existing structures, a set of publicly available tools, and a forum without preconceived outcomes that is close to the people and includes (preferably) all societal actors.

In addition, a *dense sustainability* shall be created, tried, and researched bit by bit. Numerous and diverse approaches as well as potential contributions to a sustainable development which were and are individually developed according to unique needs have to be condensed, associated, and combined to test the sustainable city in an urban transition lab. This aims at disclosing, researching, and – if possible – resolving the related interdependencies between a variety of contributions for sustainable urban development, the synergies, but also the inevitable conflicts of objectives. At the same time potentially sustainable approaches from preferably all urban areas of need and life (housing, work, supply, education, etc.) and fields of technology development (mobility, energy, protection of the environment and the climate, etc.) shall be pooled and interrelated in the project area to overcome the isolation of supposed sustainable inventions and to test them in practice in the "multi-context city".

Transdisciplinary research and the provision of KIT's benefits to the region are additional objectives of the urban transition lab. So the development process of *District Future* is a transdisciplinary one, i.e. it does not only cross the borders of individual disciplines, but also results in a collaboration of science, politics, civil society, and the private sector. This also includes the particular interest to bring science closer to the urban society – and vice versa. One the one hand, this means opening up KIT – as a knowledge factory – to the region and let the region benefit from its knowledge and skills as well. On the other hand, the actors, and here especially citizens, shall be included in knowledge generation and technology development to bring local issues, challenges, needs, and approaches concerning sustainable development into research.

3 The Integrative Concept of Sustainable Development widens the three-pillar approach of sustainability and considers not only the ecological, economic, and social dimensions, but also political-institutional and cultural aspects. The "pillars"/"dimensions" are not separated but linked and integratively considered as guidelines.

Last but not least, the establishment of the overall concept of sustainable development in urban life and the promotion of a culture of sustainability (cf. Krainer/Trattnigg 2007; Parodi 2010; Parodi et al. 2011) have to be mentioned as a target. *District Future* shall create urban life that responds to the challenges of the $21^{st}$ century with innovative technological solutions, but also quite basically with education, the revaluation of social relations, space for creativity, and adequate governance. In contrast to the common concept which associates sustainability mostly with efficiency and renouncement, *District Future* also wants to impart new qualities to urban life. The long-term establishment of the overall concept of sustainable development in all areas of urban life is imperative, providing the foundation for our actions.

Figure 2: "One meter of sustainability": The z-fold leaflet, which was designed specifically for the use in the urban transition lab, summarizes the essence of the integrative concept of sustainable development in a generally understandable way for everyday use

Source: District Future

# 5 The Project Area

The action and development of *District Future – Urban Lab* take place in Karlsruhe's Oststadt. The project area was selected after a thorough scientific analysis. In the draft phase all 27 areas of the city of Karlsruhe were assessed for their suitability as *District Future* on the basis of a pattern of ten criteria which were backed with indicators. We were neither looking for the most prosperous district, nor for the one most in need of redevelopment; we were also not interested in the one with the best development opportunities or the largest deficits regarding sustainability (distance-to-target approach), but indeed in search of the district that provided the perfect conditions for an urban transition lab: for a consolidated transdisciplinary approach that aims at the comprehensive sustainable development of a district and guarantees the transferability of as many of the results as possible. Four of the ten selection criteria were prioritized or considered more important. These are briefly described here:

(1) *"Urbanity":* The *District Future* should be one with an urban character. This criterion complies with the assessment that "the future of humanity lies in cities" (Kofi Annan[4]), and that cities as hotspots of sustainability problems on the one hand, but also of creative potential for their solutions on the other hand, are particularly interesting places of (non-)sustainability. This implies – especially once the desired model character and the transferability of *District Future* to other (European) cities is taken into account – that the district that has to be chosen should also have an urban character.

(2) *"Heterogeneity":* The aim of *District Future* is to test a holistic sustainable urban development and to pool as many different (potential) contributions to such a development as possible within a small area. Therefore the microcosm "district" should ideally reflect all aspects of urban life: Working and living, mobility and locality, consumption and production, infrastructure and quality of life, etc. However, none of these attributes should dominate the district.[5] Its population should also be heterogeneous to include and research as many different groups, affiliations, life designs, attitudes, etc. as possible.

(3) *"Potential for participation":* The urban transition lab *District Future* does not have any decision-making authority and is a far cry from having the financial framework to pursue a sustainable urban development in the project area on its own account; it only can and wants to give impetus, provide scientific guidance and therefore depends on the participation and action of the urban actors. This is the crucial point. Therefore we were looking for a district where we could at least assume and expect participation.

4 Kofi Annan at the "Conference on Sustainable Urban Development", Moscow, 5 June 2002.

5 In Karlsruhe there are explicit residential districts close to the city center.

(4) *"Proximity to the city center":* This criterion aims at two goals: On the one hand, the district should – pars pro toto – be able to represent the whole city of Karlsruhe to make it easier for Karlsruhe's citizens (and officials) to identify themselves with *District Future*, even if they do not life or act in the project area. We thus consider the acceptance within the overall structure of urban society and, in a way, also the transferability of the urban transition lab to other districts. On the other hand, the proximity to the city center also played a pragmatic role for the "commercial aspect" of the urban transition lab. Being an object of interest, the urban transition lab should be easily reachable for visitors – which is the case if it is close to the city center.

After applying the ten criteria, three districts were considered as possible project areas. They hardly differed regarding the determined characteristics and had their particular strengths and weaknesses. All three were and would be well-suited for an urban transition lab *District Future*. The decisive factor for choosing Karlsruhe's Oststadt was the vicinity to KIT. Several areas of the KIT campus can be found in the Oststadt and directly adjacent (Campus south, Campus east, a number of off-campus institutes). And since one of the aims of *District Future* is also to provide the inside, i.e. the responsible organization, with a sustainable development, the Oststadt, adjacent to KIT, was finally chosen.

The sharp (municipal) borders provide an orientation framework, but do not define strict boundaries for the urban transition lab. Projects and experiments can also be located adjacent to the Oststadt. In the end, it is not important that the interventions of sustainable urban development take place within the borders of the district (which would anyhow often equal a systemic artificial, hardly appropriate, and analytically suspect demarcation), but that they are focused within a bounded urban space, even if the boundaries are blurring.

Karlsruhe's Oststadt is an urban, heterogeneous, dense, and in many ways quite "ordinary" public space which is an adequate representative of the organically grown European city. The Oststadt has approximately 20,000 inhabitants, a high quota of migrants (32 percent) compared to the average in Karlsruhe and a population growth of 9 percent in the decade 2000-2010 (cf. Stadt Karlsruhe 2010, pp. 53-60). Due to the high proportion of younger inhabitants, especially university students, and an active (older) citizenship (e.g. organized in the local civic association and the alliance of the Oststadt's local business community [IGO]), we can assume a higher potential for participation than in other urban districts.

# 6 District Future as Urban Transition Lab

*District Future* is a typical urban transition lab since it complies with all the important characteristics that were defined in the theoretical-conceptual and, most recently, also in the scientific-political debates on the concept of urban transition labs, even though the project itself started prior to this discourse (cf. De Flander et al. 2014; Groß et al. 2005; Schneidewind 2014; Schneidewind/Scheck 2013; Wagner/Grunwald 2015). In the following we will outline how the characteristics of an urban transition lab are specified and realized in the practice of *District Future* (cf. MWK 2013, p. 30).

Figure 3: Participative elements in the urban transition lab *District Future* with reference to the participating groups of actors

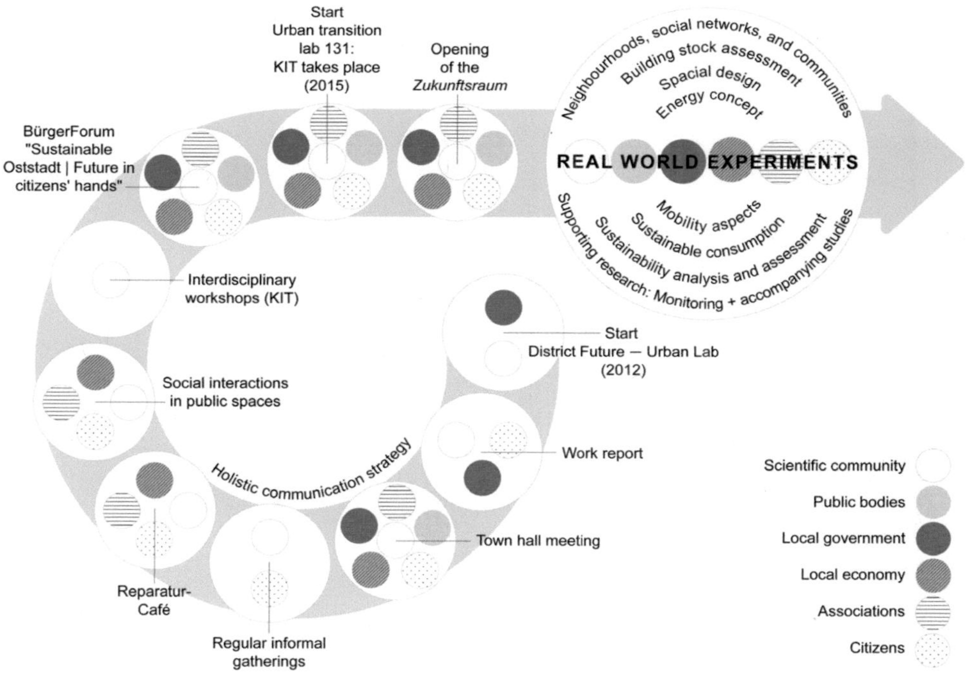


Source: District Future

### *Co-design and co-production of the research process with civil society*

Right from its beginning, *District Future* has pursued the goal to develop the thematic focus and organization of individual sub-projects and experiments with the citizens and actors in the district (cf. Parodi 2011). As an initial spark for specific, transdisciplinary projects and to agree on a thematic focus, we organized workshops[6] and two large-scale participation events: the town hall meeting "Perspectives for the Oststadt – Designing the *District Future*"[7] and the BürgerForum "Sustainable Oststadt | Future in citizens' hands"[8] (cf. Meyer-Soylu et al. 2014), which was held over several weeks. Both formats gave citizens the opportunity to voice their needs and concrete suggestions on topics relevant for sustainability like mobility, energy, neighborship, urban society, economic activities & work, and provided a platform for networking and own

Figure 4: Kick-off workshop of the BürgerForum "Sustainable Oststadt | Future in citizens' hands"

Source: District Future

6 "*District Future* first went public with a work report and a subsequent workshop for the sustainable city of the future. It presented the current status of the project development and provided insight into the project work. This was followed by the *District Future* idea workshop, where the project team discussed, drafted, and collected ideas for the sustainable city of the future with visitors in a thematically focussed way (cf. Quartier Zukunft 2013).

7 "As kick-off for *District Future – Urban Lab* in the project area Karlsruhe Oststadt the project team organized a town hall meeting 'Perspectives for the Oststadt – Designing the *District Future*' to start the dialog with the urban society in a large format" (http://quartierzukunft.de/einladung-zur-burgerversammlung-perspektive-oststadt-quartier-zukunft-gestalten/).

8 Cf. https://karlsruhe.buergerforum2014.de/.

society, economic activities & work, and provided a platform for networking and own activities. This helped to identify basic and locally relevant research fields for the urban transition lab and did not only bring people and actors together, but also advanced the development of topics – a first attempt of co-design – which have since then been and will also continue to be further elaborated over the next years in the form of transdisciplinary sub-projects ("experiments") in co-production.

### *Actors' understanding of transdisciplinary processes*

The *District Future* team attaches great importance to the transdisciplinary approach, the joint research and design on a par with actors outside the realm of science (cf. Parodi 2011). This is also communicated to its scientific partners and is a precondition for the co-operation in research projects within the framework of the urban transition lab *District Future*. Like this, the transdisciplinary approach is also conveyed to scientific disciplines which have not been familiar with this way of working so far. The transdisciplinary process understanding is realized in almost all activities of *District Future*,[9] especially in the above-mentioned sub-projects. The Karlsruhe Reparatur-

Figure 5: Some impressions from the ReparaturCafé

Source: District Future

9 Apart from transdisciplinary research there is also 'classic' (inter)disciplinary research within and of the *District Future*, e.g. the district study (cf. Hammer et al. 2014) or studies on certain aspects, like, e.g., the understanding of sustainability in the Oststadt district (cf. Waitz 2013) or the eco-system services there (cf. Albiez 2012). This disciplinary research entrenches transdisciplinary research in the corpus of classical science, accompanied and supported by transdisciplinarity.

Café, a project of *District Future*, is a good example here. Committed repairers do not only fix all sorts of damaged items there, they have also started, after some time now (to date there have been five ReparaturCafés), to contribute their own questions, reflect on their own actions in the context of sustainable development, and discuss them with the scientists in (scientific) workshops.

***Long-term guidance and layout of the research design***

*District Future* is geared to the long term, considers sustainable urban development and the related transdisciplinary research and interventions as a matter of decades rather than years. This contradicts the common time horizons of the economy, politics, research policy, and scientific practice, which creates tensions and uncertainty. However, the project team has right from the beginning been keen to get to know the project area Oststadt, to understand it completely, become acquainted, and gain the people's trust with the aim to build or allow for independent structures after all, which can then become autonomous and outlive the scientific funding as independent projects. This intensive familiarizing with the actors does not always lead to quick success, it is often rather an investment for the future. Trust needs time.

***Broad disciplinary range***

The multifaceted challenges and topics of sustainable urban development call for a multi-disciplinary team. In the core team of *District Future* alone, the following disciplines are represented: Urban geography, architecture, philosophy, cultural studies, civil engineering, environmental science, geoecology. The wider circle of those who take part in *District Future* also includes scientist working in sociology, history, political science, industrial engineering, hydraulic engineering, process engineering, electrical engineering, traffic engineering, and many others. Since the core team is located at the Institute for Technology Assessment and Systems Analysis (ITAS), there is also a broad range of disciplines close by in a scientific environment with colleagues to contact, if required. It should also be mentioned that not only transdisciplinary working, but also interdisciplinary co-operation is often a great challenge for scientists who are trained and used to work within their own discipline.

***Continuous methodical reflection***

Due to the fact that *District Future* does not only research external projects and groups, but also instigates processes, acts creatively, and initiates projects, there is also a conceptual internal perspective of the researchers involved, which requires a (particular) reflection. This reflection takes place at three levels: (a) in the form of self-reflection within the team, through mutual, sometimes also mediated exchange on the role and the purpose of one's own transdisciplinary actions; (b) in the form of a (national) scientific advisory board which was appointed by the *KIT Focus Humans and Technology* and accompanies and advises the urban transition lab *District Future*, and (c) at the level of the urban transition labs funded by the German state of Baden-Württemberg ("BaWü Labs"). As part of this funding of urban transition labs also comprehensive and supporting accompanying research is provided (cf. MWK 2015).

This accompanying research and the core team based at ITAS guarantee the *co-ordination of research support* from institutes which have experience with transdisciplinary processes in the context of the project.

# 7 Topics

In general, research in the *District Future* is carried out at two levels: a) at the level of overall urban development processes and the Oststadt district (e.g. sustainability assessment Oststadt) and b) at the level of individual transdisciplinary, topic-specific sub-projects ("real world experiments") and activities in the project area. In doing so, *District Future – Urban Lab* pays full attention to all aspects of urban life. It is committed to research and sustainable urban development in the following thematic areas:

- City and climate change
- Economic activities in the city
- Urban energy landscapes
- Mobile city
- Loop city
- Consumption in the city
- City in post–growth
- Built city
- Value shift towards sustainability
- Urban technology
- Healthy city
- Living in the city
- Design of the urban development process
- Social city

Above all, these thematic areas reflect the holistic approach of the urban transition lab. They serve primarily as an analytical pattern to make sure that no areas of urban life and important fields of sustainable development are left unnoticed. Therefore it is irrelevant that the individual thematic fields cannot be categorically differentiated and that many specified real-world experiments influence more than one thematic field. These topics are realized in the form of sub-projects (or "experiments"). The first ones started in 2014 in the project area, the sub-project "Green facades" for example operates in the thematic field "Cities and climate change", the "AG Oststadt neighbourhood"[10] in the field "Living in the city", the "Energy concept Oststadt" in "Urban en-

10 A group of citizens who organize so-called district picnics every month in the public space to foster social ties and the exchange of knowledge between the neighbours. This aims at getting to know each other better, organizing cross-generational help and exchange, and retaking possession of the public space.

ergy landscapes" or the initiated "ReparaturCafé" in the thematic fields "Loop city", "Economic activities", "Consumption", and "Post-growth". A co-operation with the Global Ecovillage Network is dedicated to the "Value shift towards sustainability". Other smaller groups deal with the topics shopping with no packaging, the establishment of a (regional) evening market for working people, or the promotion of cycling. Due to capacity constraints it is obvious that we cannot pursue all topic areas at the same time with the same intensity but have to tackle them bit by bit. These topic areas do not only have an analytical but also a considerable communicative function. Of course everyone wonders what an urban transition lab exactly contributes to sustainable urban development, which topics are specifically, or at least more specifically, dealt with.

# 8 Public Presence

*District Future – Urban Lab* depends on participation. Therefore a strong public presence and an appropriate reputation are not only helpful, but indeed necessary for a prosperous project. For the residents the clear visibility and availability in urban life, in the street, is especially important, while the municipality or other professional actors (who design the city) and the local economy are also interested in "laurels" that guarantee media attention. As examples we would like to refer to some actions *and* formats with good publicity which show the local and national public presence[11] of the urban transition lab:

- In June 2013, *District Future – Urban Lab* invited to the first work report and idea workshop in Karlsruhe to present the public with the current status of the project, to gather ideas for the further development of *District Future* with the participants of workshops on different topics of sustainable urban development, and to strengthen the network of actors for sustainable urban development in Karlsruhe.
- Since fall 2013, *District Future* has appeared in public in Karlsruhe with numerous events. The *District Future* vehicle, a cargo bike, is regularly touring the city to inform and motivate the people. Specific theme nights like "Future urban mobility" or "Regional foodstuff" take place, an OpenAir Living Room is organized, and a low-threshold invitation for the *District Future*'s group of regulars goes out to all who are interested.
- In November 2013, all residents of Karlsruhe's Oststadt received an information letter which explained the aim of the project and introduced the series of events for the kick-off in the project area in winter 2013 and spring 2014.

11 Within the science sector, the presence of the project and the interest in it go far beyond, including other European countries, Russia, Mexico, Israel, Brazil and the US.

- *District Future* received the "Deutscher Lokaler Nachhaltigkeitspreis" (German Local Sustainability Award) in the category "ZeitzeicheN-Ideen" in October 2013, a prize awarded by the Germany-wide Netzwerk21 for local sustainability.
- Since fall 2013, *District Future – Urban Lab* has been represented in the exhibition "Ideen 2020 – Ein Rundgang durch die Welt von morgen" (Ideas 2020 – A round tour of tomorrow's world) by the Helmholtz Association.
- *District Future – Urban Lab* has since 2013 been part of the urban development plan, the "Integriertes Stadtentwicklungskonzept (ISEK) Karlsruhe 2020" (integrated urban development concept).
- *District Future* invited the residents of Karlsruhe's Oststadt and all of those who are interested in sustainability in general to the town hall meeting "Perspectives for the Oststadt – Designing the *District Future*", which took place in February 2014. Approximately 200 people accepted the invitation. Together with the *District Future* team, they had a day of discussions and plans for a multitude of ideas for a sustainable urban life. Since then, these ideas have been specified.

Figure 6: Interactive map of the project area with ideas from citizens that have already been allocated after the town hall meeting "Perspectives for the Oststadt – Designing the *District Future*"

Source: KIT

- *District Future* organized the "BürgerForum Sustainable Oststadt | Future in citizens' hands", which was held at the end of 2014 in co-operation with the city of Karlsruhe. It was a multi-stage, intensive participative format which consisted of face-to-face events and a six-week online phase. About 300 people contributed to its outcome, a BürgerProgramm (citizens' program) for Karlsruhe's Oststadt (cf. Meyer-Soylu et al. 2014). The ideas that were developed there are not only considered by the municipality and urban policy, they are also taken up by *District Future* for further transdisciplinary development in the framework of the subproject "Urban transition lab 131: KIT takes place".[12]
- An interactive exhibit of *District Future* was on board the MS Wissenschaft from April 2015 until September 2015 in the framework of the Science Year 2015 "City of the Future".

# 9 Resilience and Transformation

The objective of the urban transition lab *District Future*, the transformation of an existing urban district into a sustainable one, includes – implicitly and to a certain degree also explicitly – an improved resilience to disturbances by nature or human hand, like extreme weather conditions or the impacts of socio-demographic developments ("less, more colorful, older"). There are two reasons why this resilience is particularly important for urban spaces. On the one hand, cities and urban districts are complex and compact systems of humans and their environment, sensitive structures which are prone to disturbances with sometimes dramatic consequences; on the other hand, cities hold a great potential for coping with disturbances at the same time (cf. Kegler 2015). High heterogeneity, creativity, and an established culture of participation as well as the inclusion of (local) scientific institutions can facilitate responses to and dealing with disturbances.

Resilience is also a precondition for the (permanent) sustainability of cities, because only resilient systems are able to recover from disturbances to survive in the long term (cf. Walker/Salt 2006). Therefore sustainability and resilience are closely intertwined and both are goals of, and methods, i.e. programs, for a future-oriented urban development. An urban development which is based on a broad and integrative understanding of sustainability implies and hence fosters also the development of its resilience. However, if only individual aspects of sustainability are considered in urban development, this does not contribute (systematically) to resilience, and urban development does not take advantage of its opportunities to foster resilience.

12 Cf. www.itas.kit.edu/projekte_paro15_qzrealab.php.

So a comprehensive understanding of sustainability is accompanied by a sophisticated concept of resilience which is not reduced to a system's resistance and ability to recover, but also indicates its capability for self-renewal (cf. De Flander et al. 2014; Walker/Salt 2006). Cities have to be resistant and able to withstand crises. But they also have to adapt to new circumstances, which may lead to changes and almost unpredictable further development. Thus an important element of cities' resilience is their ability to experiment or tolerate experiments and include innovations in their development (cf. Newman et al. 2009). This understanding of resilience underlines the importance of urban transition labs where experiments and innovations are realized in a transdisciplinary way and accompanied scientifically.

To illustrate the relation and interdependency between urban transition labs and resilience (cf. De Flander et al. 2014), we will link the characteristics of resilience described by Harald Kegler (cf. Kegler 2014) to concrete attributes and activities of the urban transition lab *District Future*. Kegler's characteristics are defined by opposite poles.[13]

### *Robustness and fragility*

A system with robust structures can cope well with predictable disturbances. For example, extreme rain events can be appeased by a proper greening of public spaces, one of the concerns of *District Future*. However, these robust structures have to be variable as well in order to allow adapting to different framework conditions (cf. Sieverts 2011). The climate adaption plan of the city of Karlsruhe (cf. Stadt Karlsruhe 2013) aims at such a robustness when dealing with climate change. Not only the robustness of urban planning, but also societal aspects are important here. The transdisciplinary approaches of urban transition labs for example generate socially robust knowledge which can be used by local actors in their respective contexts (cf. Groß et al. 2005). This is exactly what happens when *District Future* passes its sustainability knowledge on to the urban society, where it is contextualized and applied. At present, a consultancy on energy issues and everyday mobility is established in the district to socialize knowledge and anchor it robustly in the local urban society. Strengthening good neighborly relations within the district[14] also contributes to social robustness.

### *Compactness and decentralization*

The European district is (ideally) a compact and fragmented unit within the larger system of the city. Compact diversity allows for short distances and efficient mechanisms, for example in the field of mobility or shopping. Right from the beginning,

---

13 These poles define a field that represents the areas of action for resilience and emphasizes the transformative character of sustainable and transformative urban development.

14 Cf. http://quartierzukunft.de/ideen/.

when the project area was selected, *District Future* attached great importance to compactness in order to create a *dense sustainability* in all spheres of life. Decentralization is also a keyword, although not a magic word; if many processes and systems can be locally organized (e.g. energy production in the city block or neighborly help), others might, if applicable, also make sense in a central(ist) way (e.g. district heat supply in Karlsruhe's Oststadt). Being a lab, *District Future* also wants to provide an experimental ground for decentralized solutions where the focus was so far clearly on centralized ones; for example concepts for a local wastewater treatment and heat recovery in the city are pursued.

### *Autarky and exchange*

We can strive for autarky in many different fields, but nutrition and energy are probably the most obvious ones. However, we also have to observe (reasonable) boundaries here. A regional supply of food and local energy production often show the way to a sustainable development, but can only partially be reasonably realized in the urban space. The exchange with the "hinterland" will also remain a subject and still make sense in the city of the future. Yet it is important how this exchange and the relation between the city and the countryside are organized in terms of sustainability in a fair way. The ReparaturCafé in the *District Future* is another example for trying an approach to a self-determined life, or at least a life less determined by industry and consumption. It also illustrates the importance of social (knowledge) exchange in the urban space. Nevertheless, the boundaries and achievements of a society like ours – whose organization is mainly based on the division of labor – have to be acknowledged here as well, crazy ideas of self-sufficiency are not appropriate.

### *Redundancy and diversity*

A system consisting of diverse and redundant components can usually be considered more resistant to disturbances; it can adapt faster and easier to new situations. If ties are established to a comprehensive and integrative concept of sustainability, it becomes apparent that redundancy and diversity are addressed here, too. Also the activities initiated and accompanied by *District Future* reflect redundancy and diversity. For instance, the pending challenges of sustainable development (like "climate adaption" or "aging society") are being respectively addressed in different specific approaches in a diverse and also, to some extent, redundant way.

### *Modularity and complexity*

These opposing notions can be found in different parts of the *District Future* concept. The concept of "sustainability" as an ethical-scientific 'theory of everything' already aims at taking complexity into account (across all thematic areas, disciplines, temporal and spatial scales, societal actors, subsystems, etc.). However, the range of topics of *District Future* with its thirteen defined topic areas has a modular design (built city, healthy city, consumption in the city, loop city, mobile city, social city, etc.) to make the given complexity of urban life addressable and manageable. Apart from that, modularity and complexity of city and urban development are not an explicit characteristic of the work of *District Future*.

***Stability and flexibility***

Stability within a district does not only emerge as a result of an elaborated planning of architectural elements and infrastructures (like mixed residential districts which allow for short distances, or accessibility which makes it easier to grow old in the city), but also and above all through established social structures within the urban society. The mere composition of such structures guarantees the necessary flexibility. Solid, efficient neighbourhood networks, like, e.g., the local "Oststadt neighbours", contribute to a consolidation of the local social capital – and allow for flexibility. In this way, sound neighbourhoods are able to deal in a more flexible and resilient way with external challenges like refugees or the impacts of climate change.

[This article was first published in Hahne, U.; Kegler, H. (eds.): Resilienz. Stadt und Region – Reallabore der resilienzorientierten Transformation. Frankfurt am Main u.a.O. 2016 pp. 101–125 (in German)]

## References

Ackerman, F. (2005): Special Feature on the Environmentally Sustainable City. Material Flows for a Sustainable City. In: International Review for Environmental Strategies, Vol. 5, No. 2, pp. 499–510

Aehnelt, R.; Göbel, J.; Gorning, M.; Häußermann, H. (2009): Soziale Ungleichheit und sozialräumliche Strukturen in deutschen Städten. In: Informationen zur Raumentwicklung, No. 6, pp. 405–413 (in German)

Albiez, M. (2012): Monetäre Bewertung von Bäumen im urbanen Raum. Karlsruhe (in German)

Brake, K. (2011): "Reurbanisierung" – Globalisierung und neuartige Inwertsetzung städtischer Strukturen "europäischen" Typs. In: Frey, O.; Koch, F. (eds.): Die Zukunft der Europäischen Stadt. Stadtpolitik, Stadtplanung und Stadtgesellschaft im Wandel. Wiesbaden, pp. 299–323 (in German)

De Flander, K.; Hahne, U.; Kegler, H.; Lang, D.; Lucas, R.; Schneidewind, U.; Simon, K.-H.; Singer-Brodowski, M.; Wanner, M.; Wiek, A. (2014): Resilienz und Reallabore als Schlüsselkonzepte urbaner Transformationsforschung. Zwölf Thesen. In: GAIA – Ecological Perspectives for Science and Society, Vol. 23, No. 3, pp. 284–286 (in German)

Groß, M.; Hoffmann-Riem, H.; Krohn, W. (2005): Realexperimente. Ökologische Gestaltungsprozesse in der Wissensgesellschaft. Bielefeld (in German)

Hammer, A.; Ott, I.; Stiller, S. (2014): Karlsruhe Oststadt. Heute und in Zukunft. Überarbeiteter Entwurf. Karlsruhe (in German)

Kegler, H. (2014): Resilienz. Strategien & Perspektiven für die widerstandsfähige und lernende Stadt. Gütersloh (in German)

Kegler, H. (2015): Resilienz – neuer Maßstab für Gestaltung und Planen. In: Garten + Landschaft, No. 3, pp. 18–22 (in German)

Kopfmüller, J.; Brandl, V.; Jörissen, J.; Paetau, M.; Banse, G.; Coenen, R.; Grunwald, A. (2001): Nachhaltige Entwicklung integrativ betrachtet. Konstitutive Elemente, Regeln, Indikatoren. Berlin (in German)

Matzarakis, A. (2013): Stadtklima vor dem Hintergrund des Klimawandels. In: Gefahrstoffe – Reinhaltung der Luft, Vol. 73, No. 3, pp. 115–118 (in German)

Krainer, L.; Trattnigg, R. (eds.) (2007): Kulturelle Nachhaltigkeit. Konzepte, Perspektiven, Positionen. München (in German)

Meyer-Soylu, S.; Seebacher, A.; Albiez, M.; Bloesy, S.; Parodi, O.; Quint, A.; Waitz, C. (2014): BürgerProgramm – BürgerForum Nachhaltige Oststadt. Zukunft aus Bürgerhand. Karlsruhe (in German)

MWK – Ministerium für Wissenschaft, Forschung und Kunst Baden-Württemberg (2013): Wissenschaft für Nachhaltigkeit. Herausforderung und Chance für das Baden-Württembergische Wissenschaftssystem. Stuttgart (in German)

MWK – Ministerium für Wissenschaft, Forschung und Kunst Baden-Württemberg (2015): Begleitforschung für Reallabore in Baden-Württemberg. – URL: https://mwk.baden-wuerttemberg.de/fileadmin/redaktion/m-mwk/intern/dateien/pdf/Forschung/Reallabore/Flyer_Begleitforschung_09 Reallabore_Final.pdf [15.07.2015] (in German)

Newman, P.; Beatley, T.; Boyer, H. (2009): Resilient Cities. Responding to Peak Oil and Climate Change. Washington/DC

Parodi, O. (2010): Drei Schritte in Richtung einer Kultur der Nachhaltigkeit. In: Parodi, O.; Banse, G.; Schaffer, A. (eds.): Wechselspiele: Kultur und Nachhaltigkeit. Annäherungen an ein Spannungsfeld. Berlin, pp. 97–115 (in German)

Parodi, O. (2011): Quartier Zukunft – Labor Stadt. Projekt des KIT-Zukunftskonzepts. Karlsruhe (in German)

Parodi, O. (2015): The Missing Aspect of Culture in Sustainability Concepts. In: Enders, J. C.; Remig, M. (eds.): Theories of Sustainable Development. London/New York, pp. 169–187

Parodi, O.; Ayestaran, I.; Banse, G. (eds.) (2011): Sustainable Development – Relationship to Culture, Knowledge and Ethics. Karlsruhe

Parodi, O.; Quint, A.; Seebacher, A. (2015): Große Pläne, kleine Schritte. Die nachhaltige Stadtentwicklung des "Quartier Zukunft". In: Die Planerin, No. 2, pp. 26–28 (in German)

Quartier Zukunft (2013): Werkbericht und Ideen Workshop 2013. – URL: http://quartierzukunft.de/werkbericht-und-ideen-workshop-2013-2/ [15.07.2015] (in German)

Schneidewind, U. (2014): Urbane Reallabore – ein Blick in die aktuelle Forschungswerkstatt. In: pnd online, No. 3, pp. 1–7. – URL: http://www.planung-neu-denken.de/texte-mainmenu-41/302-schneidewind2014-3 [17.12.2015] (in German)

Schneidewind, U.; Scheck, H. (2013): Die Stadt als Reallabor für Systeminnovationen. In: Rückert-John, J. (ed.): Soziale Innovation und Nachhaltigkeit. Perspektiven sozialen Wandels. Wiesbaden, pp. 229–248 (in German)

Seebacher, A.; Albiez, M.; Parodi, O.; Quint, A.; Zimmer, S.; Walter, I. (2014): Wie Nachhaltigkeit möglich ist (Ein Leporello). Karlsruhe (in German)

Sieverts, T. (2011): Beyond Institutions? Versuch einer Positionsbestimmung der Stadtplanung. Die Bedeutung von Resilienz. In: Polis – Magazin für Urban Development, Vol. 18, No. 2, pp. 10–11 (in German)

Stadt Karlsruhe, Amt für Stadtentwicklung (2010): Stadtteilprofile Karlsruhe. Karlsruhe (in German)

Stadt Karlsruhe, Umwelt- und Arbeitsschutz (2013): Anpassung an den Klimawandel. Bestandsaufnahme und Strategie für die die Stadt Karlsruhe. Karlsruhe (in German)

Tiddens, H. (2014): Wurzeln für die lebende Stadt. Wie wir die Eigenverantwortung von Stadtteilen stärken können und warum diese mehr Wertschätzung verdienen. München (in German)

UN – United Nations, Department of Economic and Social Affairs, Population Division (ed.) (2014a): Percentage Urban and Urban Agglomerations by Size Class. – URL: http://esa.un.org/unpd/wup/Maps/CityDistribution/CityPopulation/CityPop.aspx [15.07.2015]

UN – United Nations, Department of Economic and Social Affairs, Population Division (ed.) (2014b): World Urbanization Prospects. The 2014 Revision. Highlights. New York

Wagner, F.; Grunwald, A. (2015): Reallabore als Forschungs- und Transformationsinstrument. Die Quadratur des hermeneutischen Zirkels. In: GAIA – Ecological Perspectives for Science and Society, Vol. 24, No. 1, pp. 26–31 (in German)

Waitz, C. (2013): Nachhaltigkeit in der Stadt. Eine empirische Untersuchung zur Identifikation der Bedeutung von Nachhaltigkeit am Beispiel der Stadt Karlsruhe. Karlsruhe (in German)

WBGU – Wissenschaftlicher Beirat der Bundesregierung Globale Umweltveränderungen (1996): Welt im Wandel – Herausforderung für die deutsche Wissenschaft. Bremerhaven (in German)

Walker, B.; Salt, D. (2006): Resilience Thinking. Sustaining Ecosystems and People in a Changing World. Washington/DC

# Local Citizen Participation in the European Context

*Albert Geiger*

Europe is undergoing change, it is changing ever more rapidly, and the relationships are becoming increasingly complex. In Germany, we will lose nearly 17 million inhabitants in the next 30 years, according to the latest forecasts. Every third person in this country will be 65 or older by then. The number of students will be halved in the next 30 years. The energy transition must be achieved. For a European city, it is more than ever important to find answers to the crucial questions of the future.

## 1 "We are they and they are we!"

In practice, there is no clear path with a sign at the beginning that reads: "This takes you directly to the simple answer to complex questions about the future." In fact, there are many ways. Most of them are neither mapped nor prepared for a navigation system. In order to find the way forward for Ludwigsburg, in 2004 the city administration and city council embarked on a journey towards finding the right coordinates. We called this journey "Opportunities for Ludwigsburg". In the following, we put emphasis on broad citizen participation. The city designed the future program in a two-year process with more than 1,000 participants.

Master plans were designed for key issues such as education, integration, energy, culture, work, and economy. This is a tedious task that promises fewer headlines than announcing prestigious construction projects. When more citizens overcome the inertia of the mass and get involved, we all benefit; this dispels mistrust and builds more trust among the actors. It is no longer about those at the top who do what they want anyway. The new slogan is "We are they and they are we." The power struggles about tax distribution and consolidation contributions must give way to a strategically coordinated and jointly supported financial policy based on intergenerational equity. Political decisions at the local level tend to become more factual. Individual decisions can be more effectively integrated into overall strategies and priorities.

Ludwigsburg's policy approach thus gives access to the creative ideas of the citizens. They identify more closely with their city. They get involved in an incredible number of ways and contribute to the challenges of drawing up intergenerationally equitable budgets. The principle is: "The sustainable city does not charge the future." The sustainable urban development policy is in line with the objectives of the Rio Conference in 1992. The initiatives and developments that have emerged in many cities since then are an integral part of the sustainable urban development with intensive citizen participation.

Since this is not only a local but also a national and international issue, Ludwigsburg decided in 2005 – during the hottest phases of citizen participation in the urban development concept – to take part in the European project called Managing Urban Europe (MUE) (2005-2008). In this project, 25 European cities worked intensively on developing successful participation, management tools, and a method for long-term sustainable urban development. During the project, the actors in the Ludwigsburg city administration realized that cities in Europe have much to learn from each other in terms of successful citizen participation. At this time, Brussels had already approached the local authorities and promoted the involvement of people in shaping the future using participatory approaches.

So it was a matter of ensuring that these findings would be reflected in practical administrative action in the future. The management cycle in the MUE project offers European cities and municipalities a tool to institutionalize citizen participation in the development and maintenance of the programs for the future regardless of events. In 2007, during the German EU Council Presidency, the Leipzig Charter on Sustainable European Cities set out important guidelines towards this end. For understandable reasons, the strategies defined therein became a prerequisite for access to communal EU and partly national funding programs. According to the logic of horizontally networked policy at the local level, such networking must also take place at the regional, national and European levels. The same logic shows that the policies from the community up to the EU also need to be better integrated vertically. Given the current financial crisis and imminent state bankruptcies in the EU as well as the already partially incapacitated municipalities, this, in particular, presents a substantial opportunity and responsibility.

## 2 Processes of Change

During the projects above, we made organizational changes to better manage overall urban development planning processes. These were aimed at shaping the future in line with the expectations of the citizens. "With the world becoming more complex, more brains need to think" is the guiding principle of this idea. The Department for Sustainable Urban Development was established in 2008, responsible for managing change processes and the integration of various fields of action. Based on the findings and due to the exceptionally positive experience in the project Managing Urban Europe, Ludwigsburg has since participated in a large number of European funding programs. Some of them focus on the topic of participation in the European context. Urgent challenges of the future, such as energy and climate protection, generally play a key role here. In autumn 2010, for example, the European project MUSIC (Mitigation in Urban Areas) was launched. The total budget of 5.62 million euros is distributed among seven project partners: the cities of Ludwigsburg, Rotterdam, Ghent, Montreux and Aberdeen, and two research institutes. The project deals with the question of how to achieve the energy transition in the cities and significantly reduce $CO_2$ emissions using new approaches and instruments. The focus is on three areas:

- *Transition management* – an innovative method of citizen participation, which was developed by the project partner DRIFT (Dutch Research Institute for Transitions of the University of Rotterdam) and is used in the partner cities of the project.
- *Urban energy maps* summarizing various information on energy in a geographic information system (in collaboration with the project partner Research Institute Henri Tudor)
- *Pilot projects* in the partner cities of the project: high-quality, energy-efficient public buildings with high visitor numbers.

In Ludwigsburg, the “local energy transition” process was launched as part of the transition management. In a first step, a project team was formed within the city administration. In addition to the project managers from the Department for Sustainable Urban Development, the Department of Civic Engagement was involved with a focus on citizen participation and energy issues. The team jointly selected citizens of Ludwigsburg who in fall 2011 were interviewed about the urban development process, sustainable energy supply, and possibilities for citizen participation in Ludwigsburg. Among the 30 respondents were members of the municipal council, energy experts and interested laypersons. The aim was to stimulate enthusiasm for the process among so-called “front runners”, that is, people who think outside the box, who are creative and committed to dealing with new issues and promoting them.

The innovative approach of “transition management” (the management of change) is not to invite to a broad participatory process, but to start with a small group of selected “front runners.” Later, the process will be re-expanded to involve more actors. In November 2011, all respondents were invited to a kick-off meeting where the main results of the interviews were presented. They provided very interesting insights into the various areas considered. The findings were then incorporated into the process with the interested “front runners.” Until September 2012, seven meetings were held with ten to fifteen participants each.

# 3 Thematic Links

After taking stock of the issue of energy in Ludwigsburg, the group identified primary urban development topics that could be linked together – from housing, education, culture and green spaces to mobility and energy issues. It was interesting to see that energy is involved in all aspects of daily life – where we live, what we buy, how we move, where we recover, etc. The participants then jointly developed a vision "One day in the life of Ludwig and Ludwiga in 2050".[1] In the next step, they looked at various topics such as consumption, recycling, and energy saving in buildings, and discussed from the perspective of 2050 what needs to happen by 2030, 2020, 2015 and today to make this vision a reality. Based on this, practical recommendations and ideas were formulated and reconciled, resulting in an agenda of who and what is needed to put these measures into practice. The results achieved were then discussed at the "energy roundtable" with around 60 politicians, citizens and other stakeholders. In an "energy café," various topics such as "green in the city," "feel-good railway station," "innovative energy supply," and "sustainable consumption" were discussed.

The results from the "energy roundtable" were discussed at the City's fourth Conference on the Future in November 2012, taking into account of other issues and developing ideas such as "face-to-face energy advice" or "energy exhibition". Here, connections to the EU project "Livinggreen" became obvious. This project aims to develop "Energy Info Centers" in the project's partner cities, which offer innovative advice on the renovation of buildings, saving energy, energy efficiency, and renewable energy. As part of the project, Ludwigsburg plans to establish an exhibition on energy, together with Energetikom – Center for Energy Competence and Eco Design and the Public Library in the cultural center of Ludwigsburg. At the end of 2012, the entire "local energy transition" process was posted on the newly launched citizen participation platform "MeinLB.de" (www.meinlb.de) as a project. In February 2013, all those involved and other interested persons were invited to an "Energy Market of Opportunities" in order to develop concrete projects to be implemented by and with citizens based on their ideas, suggestions and visions. Several energy projects are going to be realized soon – ranging from a tree of books with literature on sustainability and a car-free week with celebrities as role models.

# 4 European Exchange of Experience

The exchange of experience with other European cities plays an important role for Ludwigsburg, such as in the project EnSURE (Energy Savings in Urban Quarters

1 Editors' note: "Ludwig and Ludwiga" is a synonym of "male and female residents of Ludwigsburg".

through Rehabilitation and New Ways of Energy Supply). The aim of this project is to improve urban energy balances by developing integrated approaches and implementing pilot projects on energy-efficient renovation of buildings, renewable energy, mobilization of owners to improve the urban energy balances, and innovative financing instruments. To this end, the 13 partners from Germany, Hungary, Italy, Poland, and Slovenia will exchange experiences and support projects for sustainable urban development. One focus is on the development of approaches in which the respective energy projects are embedded. This is particularly important as in Europe individual measures are still too often implemented without reference to an overall strategy. In the European project EnSURE, Ludwigsburg, the lead partner of this project, brought its experience in integrated urban development to the European partnership, based on the city-wide integrated urban development concept. In Ludwigsburg, the district and quarter level was considered in more detail. Using a specially developed energy strategy, a concept of energy-efficient renovation was developed for a typical post-war quarter.

The concepts include retrofitting scenarios, a follow-up study, new concepts of energy supply, and implementation strategies. In addition, strategies have been developed to encourage owners and tenants as well as key stakeholders such as energy suppliers and housing associations to cooperate in the process. An important outcome of the project is that the major players must necessarily be involved from the beginning of the process. The pilot energy project is integrated into the ongoing development process in the district (development plan "Oststadt"). Energy issues can thus be discussed along with other aspects as part of an iterative and integrated approach.

These examples demonstrate that a citizens' Europe can only succeed if the cities and municipalities engage in dialogue with the public based on committed participation and communicate European issues to their citizens as partners of Brussels. The change in mentality introduced with the Leipzig Charter, which can also be described as a cultural change, is an excellent opportunity to do so. Brussels wants to reach out to the citizens. They are supposed to shape Europe. This will only succeed if the two lower rungs of the ladder leading to the people are stable and solid. These rungs are the municipalities. They play a key role. They are the ones who must successfully design citizen participation. Thus, from the perspective of local, regional, state and federal but also European policy, there are no alternatives for successful participation.

# The Sustainable City in Romania

## From Vision to Reality

*Ildiko Tulbure*

## 1 The Concept of Sustainable Development and its Operationalisation

In a time of major technological developments on a global level starting in the 1970's and 80's, the world began to monitor select dangers and undesired effects of human activities, especially industrial ones. After the *Conference for Environment* in Stockholm in 1972 and the first report of the Club of Rome, "The Limits to the Growth" in 1972 (cf. Meadows 1972), it was understood that besides the positive effects of technological progress, undesired and negative effects can also appear. After this time, environmental awareness in the Western world increased. It was clear that the many regional and global environmental problems are very serious and need to be solved. We now confront a series of global problems which can be grouped into three categories: the increase of natural resource and energy consumption, environmental pollution, and the increase in world population (cf. Jischa 2014) (see Figure 1)

Global discussions began on political, scientific and social scales in order to find solutions to the problems above which could be applicable in developed as well as developing countries. The *Brundtland Report* of the World Commission on Environment and Development represented a prominent result of these worldwide discussions. For the first time the concept of *sustainable development* was defined in this report and accepted as a possible global approach to complex new ecological, economic, and social problems (cf. Brundtland 1987).

The concept of sustainable development was discussed more often thereafter, as in 1992 at the Conference on Environment and Development in Rio de Janeiro, and was strongly emphasised in the conference's resulting document *Agenda 21*, as well as during the 2002 follow-up conference Rio+10 in Johannesburg, South Africa (cf. Tulbure 2013). Since then many similar scientific consensuses have found that the evolution of technical, social and ecological systems must be analysed in synergistic relation to one another (cf. Jischa 2014).

Figure 1: Global (Environmental) Problems and the Concept of Sustainable Development with its Operationalisation

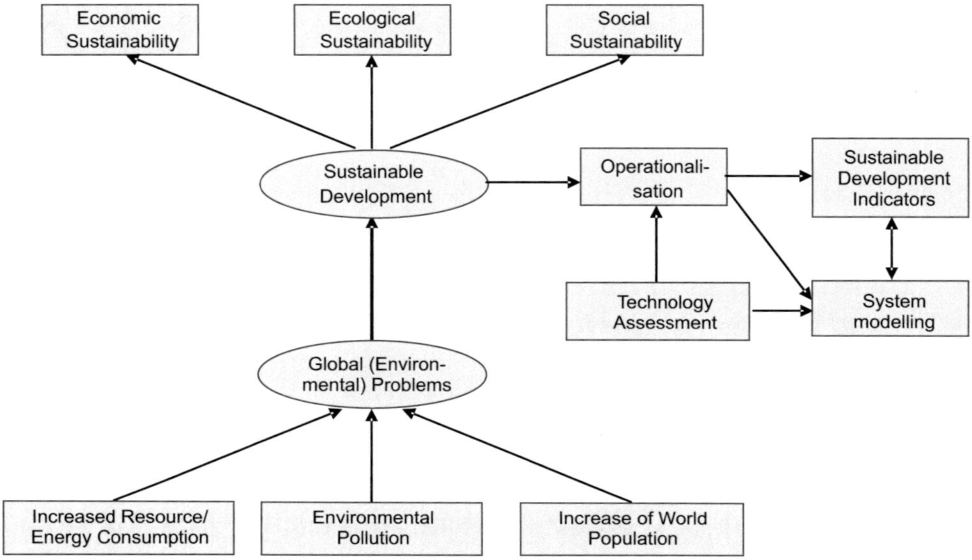


Author's Archive

Sustainable development has become a more widely used term today. However, perusal of related literature gives the impression that there are as many definitions of sustainable development as there are users of the term (cf. Banse et al. 2011). In order to make this concept more understandable, rules, strategies and principles of sustainable development have been defined (cf. Jischa 2014; Tulbure 2003). The general Brundtland definition has been accepted world-wide , but together with the rules, strategies and principles, it does not deliver a concrete methodology on resolving how to apply the concept of sustainable development to actual and specific situations, especially on local or even finer levels (cf. Parodi et al. 2010; Tulbure 2013).

The operationalisation of sustainable development means the translation of its goals into political measures and controlling instruments (cf. Jischa 2014; Lengsfeld et al. 2003). A general methodology for the operationalisation of sustainable development can be materialised in the following steps (cf. Tulbure 2003):

- defining the sustainability problem;
- establishing specific space and time scales;
- a systemic approach to the region by modeling the interactions therein;
- establishing concrete aims for the studied example by establishing priorities;

- developing evaluation and control instruments, e.g. indicators;
- verifying the possible results obtained after introducing the proposed measures;
- applying the developed concept into practice.

The operationalisation is only possible when for an individual problem or case, concrete aims are established and from these aims, concepts to achieve them are developed (cf. Schauer 2000). Sustainability is to be newly defined for each different case. The space and time scales are to be established specific to each case (cf. Banse et al. 2011; Tulbure 2011).

Strategic possibilities for the operationalisation of sustainable development include:

(1) Establishing goals on a global scale, the measures to achieve these goals being prepared on global and national levels and applied at regional levels.
(2) Establishing goals on regional levels, the measures being prepared on regional levels and immediately applied; the effects of these measures are to be evaluated on national and global levels, as well.

An example of the first strategy is the goal of finding future sustainable energy supply systems with minimal effects on the environment. Such a project has been realized at the IIASA (International Institute for Applied Systems Analysis) in Laxenburg/Vienna, "Globale Energieperspektiven bis 2050 und darüber hinaus". The IKARUS project (Instruments for Reducing Emissions of Gases relevant to Climatic Changes) developed by several institutes in Germany represents another example (cf. Tulbure 2003). These studies are based on mathematical models to describe industrial and economic processes. With the help of a database which describes economic, social and political components, simulations have been created and different development scenarios are explored. The goal is to identify ways for the proposed aims to help with the political decision making process by providing concrete data measures (cf. Banse et al. 2011).

The second strategy has seen applications as well, such as in Local Agenda 21, especially in Western Europe following the Rio-Conference in 1992. There are numerous national studies which endeavor to find ways for nations to develop sustainably within the global context, such as the action plan "Sustainable Netherlands" by Friends of Earth Netherlands in 1992 or the study, "Zukunftsfähiges Deutschland" (Sustainable Germany), initiated by BUND (Friends of Earth – Association for Environment and Nature Protection) and Misereor and lead by the Wuppertal Institute for Climate, Environment and Energy (cf. BUND/Misereor 1996).

With the goal of executing the second strategy for operationalisation of sustainable development on regional levels, in 2006 the Network for Sustainability Strategies, Monitoring and Management in Southeastern Europe was established. This event took place in the context of a kick-off conference held in Romania, at the 1 Decembrie

1918 University in the city of Alba Iulia, and sponsored by the German Academic Exchange Service, DAAD (cf. Tulbure/Jischa 2006). In order to achieve best results with the launching of the new Network for Sustainability in Southeastern Europe, this conference was scientifically and organisationally assisted by several German partners, especially the Clausthal University of Technology, represented at the event by professor Dr.-Ing. M. Jischa, as well as the Institute for Technology Assessment and Systems Analysis, ITAS, of the Karlsruhe Institute of Technology, KIT, represented at the event by Dr. G. Banse. One frequently discussed strategy for sustainable development operationalisation during this event was in finding solutions for future sustainable energy supply systems on national and regional levels (cf. Tulbure 2014; Tulbure/Jischa 2006).

The field of developing future energy systems is currently debated on many organizational and governmental levels with the goal of assuring the sustainability of society. Present discussions regarding existing regional strategies for arranging optimal future energy systems are led by the goal of mitigating harmful effects of climate change (cf. Mueller/Lindeman 2013; Parodi et al 2010).

Part of what engineers do is to evaluate developments in technology; their evaluations have until now almost exclusively focused on technical aspects, like functionality and safety, and on economic, legally and financially limiting conditions (cf. Jischa 2014). With respect to sustainability more criteria have to be considered, such as environmental resource quality, social and human values, and quality of life (cf. Banse et al. 2011; Lengsfeld et al. 2003; Mueller/Lindeman 2011). Performing these types of evaluations requires interdisciplinary cooperation (Parodi et al. 2010). In order to support the activities of engineers when evaluating technologies a new discipline emerged, first in the USA, which combines different aspects of emerging technologies and perspectives on their use, called Technology Assessment (TA) (cf. Grunwald 2012; Jischa 2014; Tulbure 2013). TA means the methodical, systematic, organised process of:

- analysing a technology and its developmental possibilities,
- assessing the direct and indirect technical, economic, health, ecological, social and other impacts of this technology and possible alternatives,
- judging these impacts according to defined goals and values, and determining future goals,
- deriving possibilities for action and design and expanding upon these.

Well-founded decisions are more likely to be made and implemented by the appropriate institutions with the use of TA (cf. VDI 1991).

When reviewing the given methodology for operationalising sustainable development, one can recognise that many steps useful to this methodology can be also identified in the phases described by TA (cf. Tulbure 2013; Tulbure/Jischa 2006). Often a concrete sustainability problem, especially related to a technological issue, can be addressed by carrying out a TA study.

On the global level, the operationalisation of sustainable development requires the definition of general goals for the whole world, as was attempted with the Rio-Conference and the better-known Kyoto Protocol. On a national level this requires the definition of goals and expansion of specific strategies according to the specific conditions of a country, as variances in national conditions require. This aspect is especially applicable to the social and cultural fields, where national particularities can be very different from one country to another (cf. Banse et al. 2011). On regional or local scales, measures taken usually represent those associated with Local Agendas 21, but this is not always the case, as there are still discussions in different parts of the world, as in Southeast Europe, on how to apply optimal conditions for sustainable development on regional or local scales (cf. Tulbure/Jischa 2006).

## 2 Urban Sustainability – Methodological Aspects

The practice of applying sustainable development on a local level (in order to achieve so-called urban sustainability) represents a fairly new direction for some countries in Southeast Europe (cf. Banse et al. 2011). More specifically, the operationalisation of sustainable development on the scale of companies or of industrial processes is a relatively new and interesting field (cf. Schauer 2000; Tulbure 2014).

Nevertheless, the field of urban sustainability is just beginning in Romania, as is generally the case throughout Southeast Europe (cf. Banse et al. 2011; Tulbure 2011). An appropriate means for developing strategies for urban sustainability could be achieved by using the analytical instruments of Technology Assessment, because very often the questions which arise through its methodology relate to the possibilities for the optimal integration of new technologies on local levels into the environment and society. These questions arise from present conditions in Eastern European countries which dominant political importance, relating to the process of modernisation of old technologies and implementation of new ones. For this reason TA should play a central role in the future technological, economic, environmental and social development of these countries (cf. Grunwald 2010; Jischa 2014; Tulbure 2013).

The importance of assuring urban sustainability has been pointed out by the UN Habitat Executive Director, Dr. J. Clos, who recognised during a UN Habitat Conference that there is "no sustainable development without sustainable urbanisation". Furthermore, the vision of having future *sustainable cities*, by taking into account regional differences, is frequently discussed worldwide, but has also started to be debated in some Eastern European countries (cf. Banse et al. 2011; Tulbure 2011).

Discussions have begun in Romania, especially among scientific communities, on how to achieve future *sustainable cities* and establish a general methodology for this goal in accordance with the already developed and applied methodologies in other European countries by taking into consideration specific differences, especially on social and cultural levels (cf. Banse et al. 2011). In this regard, by applying the sustainability systemic analysis on a local level (cf. Tulbure 2003), the general methodology for *sustainable urbanisation* can be gleaned and actualized through the following steps:

- defining the sustainability problems on a local/regional level;
- establishing specific space and time scales;
- establishing concrete aims for the case in question;
- developing a systemic, region-specific approach by modeling interactions;
- developing concepts and measures by establishing priorities;
- developing evaluation and control instruments;
- verifying the possible results by measuring them after introducing the proposed measures, and by developing appropriate scenarios;
- applying the resulting concepts.

When analysing this methodology for sustainable urbanisation, one can recognise that "urban sustainability" refers to a transformation process under variable frame conditions, as is the general discussion regarding sustainability operationalisation (cf. Tulbure 2003). *Urban sustainability management*, as presented in Figure 2, emphasises development at the local level. This is accomplished by simultaneously considering economic, ecological and social aspects and representing them on the axes, as shown in Figure 2, by using relevant indicators for each considered field. The evaluation of the development path is possible, if desired (D) and undesired (U) ranges can be defined for each considered aspect, as shown in Figure 2. If the development is situated in the so-called "sustainable action range", this means urban sustainability will be assured. If the development is situated in the so-called "unsustainable range", development corrections can be made by introducing measures with the end of achieving urban sustainability, as emphasised in Figure 2.

This methodology is generally to be applied on a local or regional level, without any restrictions, but special attention must be paid to the following possible difficulties (cf. Jischa 2014; Tulbure 2003):

- The processes are complex and can contain uncertainties.
- There is a need to integrate quantitative as well as qualitative aspects into the analysis.
- If none exist, it is necessary to design indicators for urban sustainability, in order to succeed in evaluating development over time.

Figure 2: Urban Sustainability Management

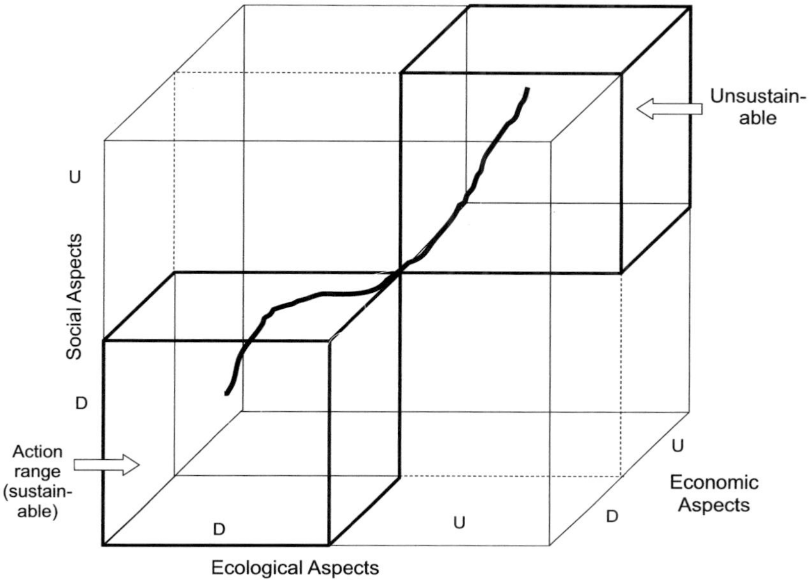


Author's Archive

# 3 The Concept of Decoupling

Several newly discussed strategies for sustainable urban development have at their base the concept of "decoupling", a relatively new term in sustainability literature. It was mentioned by the Club of Rome during its Conference "Governance of the Commons", that took place in September 2013 in Ottawa, Canada (cf. Tulbure 2014). The discussion intended to rejuvenate the global debate on *Limits to Growth* (cf. Meadows 1972), and sustainable development, climate change and questions of equity.

Decoupling typically refers to the aim of breaking the long-held causal relationship between economic growth and growth in the consumption of natural resources. The essence of decoupling means to assure a high quality of life for all citizens in the world, but without rampant growth in energy consumption, with all its impacts on the environment and other resources. Decoupling goes beyond simple price adjustments or marginal policy shifts but strikes a blow at the heart of the fundamental yet mistaken belief that economic growth and natural resource use are two sides of the same coin, joined forever in a mutually reinforcing bind. Those who advocate decoupling believe that the binding knot can, and must be broken.

It is understood as a viable strategy for assuring the sustainability of our society. It has relevance both for developing and developed countries, allowing us to release the dependence of our well-being from that of the consumption of the limited treasures of the Earth. This can be supported by a massive investment in technological and social innovation, so that at least the per capita energy and resource consumption in developed countries will not increase further. Likewise, it is important to support developing countries in following a more sustainable development path. By using this fairly new direction in an optimal manner on local scales, with other strategies for social applications, it would be possible to take important steps for assuring urban sustainability.

# 4 Sustainable Cities in Romania: Examples

Regarding the situation in Romania, a currently debated question is how to transform a city in Romania into a regional or local model of sustainable development, into a sustainable city (cf. CC 2011). After joining the European Union in 2007, the word "sustainability" started to be heard more frequently in Romania. New opportunities for people to explore and learn from Western countries were suddenly opened up. Since then only small steps have been taken, sometimes because of bureaucracy, sometimes because of competing priorities, and sometimes because of lack of knowledge and lack of financial resources. Nevertheless, in the last several years some progress has been registered in the field of sustainable urban development (cf. CC 2011).

In order to emphasize this development, Sibiu, selected in 2007 to become the European Capital of Culture, and the five biggest cities in Romania will be considered: Bucharest, Cluj-Napoca, Timisoara, Iasi and Constanta. In order to become sustainable cities, they all share certain needs (cf. CC 2011):

- urban regeneration;
- reduced energy consumption;
- more transportation options other than cars.

The Romanian Government approved in 2009 a program for the rehabilitation of residential urban buildings constructed between 1950 and 1990. There were four major benefits from this action plan:

- increasing the energy efficiency of the buildings;
- changing the facades;
- protecting the environment by reducing emissions;
- subsidizing money spent by building owners, e.g., through specific programmes it became possible to obtain funding from national and local governments for rehabilitation.

Also, the idea of constructing green buildings has very much come into discussion, as in the city of Cluj-Napoca. This city has the first "Green School" of Romania, established in 2012. The following savings have been registered for this building:

- energy savings: 30%;
- water savings: 50%;
- waste savings: 50–90%.

In this context, starting in 2013, the construction of green buildings has been encouraged by Romanian local authorities, for example by reducing local taxes for them by 50%.

Currently there are also discussions in the field of alternative transportation options. The populations of several cities agree that bicycles will need to be used more frequently. The largest bike-sharing project in the country was launched in 2010 in Bucharest, followed in 2011 by Cluj-Napoca and Constanta as well as by Timisoara in 2012. Each city is hoping that this initiative will help reduce their carbon footprint and sustain the development of an adequate infrastructure for cyclists (cf. CC 2011).

Another newly discussed strategy is based on the usage of bioenergies and biotechnologies, in order to establish future energy strategies for sustainable urban development (cf. Jischa 2005; Tulbure 2014). Bioenergy is a renewable energy made available from materials derived from biological sources, such as biomass. Biotechnologies use combinations of engineering processes with biological methods, based on microorganisms.

Taking into consideration the use of biotechnologies alongside the strategy of decoupling, these two newer directions, in a proper combination with other strategies for social application, would assist progress towards urban sustainability in Romania.

# 5 Sustainable Development Strategy of the Romanian Region Alba

The Alba Iulia Association for Intercommunity Development (AIDA)[1] is a Romanian non-governmental organisation representing the interests of three urban and eight rural communities. This association of eleven local administrative units represents the interests of more than 120,000 inhabitants. AIDA aims to encourage economic and social development on a regional level through varied actions.

With approximately 66,000 inhabitants, Alba Iulia is the most important city in the association, and is symbolic of Romania's history. Alba Iulia has a development strategy that aims to acknowledge optimal urban governance as a positive force in improving housing standards, equity and sustainability standards.

1 Cf. http://www.albaiulia-aida.ro/.

The city's Strategic Development Plan is designed to address issues related to improving the quality of pedestrian and public areas, and also to improve accessibility to the historic fortress area, which is a major tourism landmark. The environmental policy of Alba Iulia also targets transportation issues as they relate to the city's relatively well-developed tourism industry (cf. CC 2011).

AIDA has several strategic objectives with the vision of improving the quality of life in the region (cf. CC 2011):

1. developing the local and regional infrastructure;
2. making economic progress by developing new jobs;
3. capitalizing on the anthropic and natural tourist potential;
4. promoting "green energy";
5. promoting the local cultural values and traditions;
6. improving the educational, social and health infrastructure;
7. building regional, national or international partnerships.

In this strategy for sustainable development, several aspects will be necessary for future sustainable development of this region:

(a) the need for transnational cooperation in encouraging sustainable urban development;
(b) holistic education in urban sustainability;
(c) establishing a general model of a Romanian sustainable city.

The *need for transnational cooperation* has long been recognised by the Network for Sustainability Strategies, Monitoring and Management in South Eastern Europe at the 1 Decembrie 1918 University in Alba Iulia (cf. Tulbure/Jischa 2006). Such cooperation, especially via projects in sustainability monitoring in Southeast Europe, as well as in the field of university sustainability education in Southeast Europe, can have major impacts.

The field of holistic education for urban sustainability has an important goal in attempting to change public opinion and ways of thinking, as education is the key to achieving sustainability! In his book "Continuity, Innovation and Change", HRH Prince Hassan, former President of the Club of Rome, pointed out the need for education as a key issue for achieving three human goals: *continuity, innovation, and change*. These are the fundaments of sustainable development of our society, and are accomplished by taking into account regional differences. Three dimensions of education must be recognised: infrastructure, methodologies and values.

Establishing a *general profile of a Romanian sustainable city* is essential and demonstrative of the principal that sustainability can only function when tailored to each region. In applying this concept there is a need to evaluate systems in an integrated way, from technical, economic, environmental and social points of view. There are various major problems regarding urban sustainability in different parts of the world;

this means that specific regional conditions have to be taken into consideration. From this aspect it follows that there is a need to develop a general profile of a Romanian sustainable city, by taking into account local-scale conditions.

# 6 Conclusions

It should be mentioned that presently there is no consensus regarding a general definition for a Romanian sustainable city nor is there consensus upon a paradigm for what components should be included in this concept. Generally there is agreement that a sustainable city should meet the needs of the present without compromising the ability of future generations to meet their own needs. The inherent ambiguity and paradox within this idea leads to a great deal of variation in terms of how cities carry out their attempts to become sustainable. However, a sustainable city should be able to feed itself with minimal reliance on the surrounding countryside, and power itself with renewable sources of energy.

Today the goal is to generally promote the idea of achieving sustainable regions, not only sustainable cities, by taking into account all aspects related to this issue such as: technical, economic, social and environmental aspects as they relate to adequate living conditions and housing space, efficient resource use, transportation, governance and culture. This means that there is a real need for interdisciplinary work among economists, engineers and social scientists. Developing a general methodology to be applied in practice for real situations by considering regional differences would represent a major advancement in this field and aid progress from the vision to the reality.

To effectively apply present developments in the field of sustainable urban development, it would be useful for Romanian cities to become partners in international networks of sustainable cities, to learn from the experiences of other cities in other countries and to cooperate on emerging trends in sustainable urban development. The objective is to find appropriate ways to implement strategies for sustainable urban development in Romania and to establish a general profile for a *Romanian sustainable city*.

## References

Banse, G.; Nelson, G.; Parodi, O. (eds.) (2011): Sustainable Development – The Cultural Perspective. Concepts – Aspects – Examples. Berlin

Brundtland, G. H. (ed.) (1987): Our Common Future. The Brundtland Report to the World Commission on Environment and Development. Oxford.

BUND/Misereor (eds.) (1996): Zukunftsfähiges Deutschland. Basel (in German)

CC – City Council (2011): Sustainable Development Strategy of the Alba Region AIDA. Alba Iulia (Municipal Council)

Grunwald, A. (2010): Technikfolgenabschätzung. Eine Einführung (2nd ed.). Berlin (in German)

Jischa, M. F. (2014): Herausforderung Zukunft. Berlin a.o. (in German)

Lengsfeld, T.; Tulbure, I.; Ali, V. (eds.) (2003):Exploring a Worthwhile Future for All. A Report of tt30 of the Club of Rome. Valencia (Spanish Chapter of the Club of Rome)

Meadows, D.; Meadows, D. (1972): The Limits to Growth. New York

Mueller, E.; Lindeman, K. (2011): Climate Change in Several Central and South American Ecosystems. In: Banse, G.; Nelson, G.; Parodi, O. (eds.): Sustainable Development – The Cultural Perspective. Concepts – Aspects – Examples. Berlin, pp. 339–348

Parodi, O.; Banse, G.; Schaffer, A. (eds.) (2010): Wechselspiele: Kultur und Nachhaltigkeit. Annäherungen an ein Spannungsfeld. Berlin (in German)

Schauer, T. (2000): Lifestyles, Future Technologies and Sustainable Development. Ulm (FAW – Forschungsinstitut für anwendungsorientierte Wissensverarbeitung)

Tulbure, I. (2003):Integrative Modellierung zur Beschreibung von Transformationsprozessen. Habilitationsschrift. TU Clausthal. Düsseldorf (VDI-Fortschrittsberichte, Reihe 16, Nr. 154) (in German)

Tulbure, I.; Jischa, M. F. (2006): First Report on Activities of the Network for Sustainability Strategies, Monitoring and Management in South-Eastern Europe (NESSEE). Bonn (DAAD – German Academic Exchange Service)

Tulbure, I. (2011): Considerations Regarding Cultural Differences when Operationalising Sustainability on Regional Level. In: Banse, G.; Nelson, G.; Parodi, O. (eds.): Sustainable Development – The Cultural Perspective. Concepts – Aspects – Examples. Berlin, pp. 125–135

Tulbure, I. (2013): Technikbewertung. Vorlesungsskript. Clausthal-Zellefeld (TU Clausthal)

Tulbure, I. (2014): Assessing Biotechnologies for Environmental Protection. In: Conference Proceedings, SIMPRO 2014. Petrosani (University of Petrosani), pp. 135–140

VDI – Verein Deutscher Ingenieure (1991): VDI-Richtlinie 3780 "Technikbewertung – Begriffe und Grundlagen". Düsseldorf (VDI – Verein Deutscher Ingenieure) (in German)

# Peri-Urban Villages of Bangalore, India

## Reclaiming the Commons to Cope with Climate Stress and Unsustainable Resource Utilization Systems

*Appakuttan Damodaran, Tanushree Haldar*

## 1 Backdrop

Mundur is a village spanning an area of 1,302 acres. This village is located towards the east of Bangalore, India, 26 km away from the city's centre. Prior to the 1980s, the village had a historically diverse set of common property resources and common grazing grounds, water bodies and tree groves accounting for roughly 27% of the village's geographic area. The village enjoys an average annual precipitation of about 720 mm and is vulnerable to periodic droughts. Traditionally, it was a symbiotic man-livestock relationship and a subsistence-based cropping system that had saved Mundur from the deprivation and impacts of droughts (cf. Damodaran 1993). The symbiotic relationship was enabled by a community-driven land use system that permitted the village livestock to be grazed in common grass lands during monsoons and water bodies during summer months and then over-harvested fields (belonging to farmers) during winter months. Thus, the grazing regimes available in the village included not only common property resources (CPR) but also private property resources (PPR).

The advent of commercial farming in the village in the 1980s and the externalities of solid waste pollution from Bangalore city by the turn of this century caused resource utilization systems to deviate from traditional land use systems which were based on sustainable utilisation of land resources.

The new resource utilisation modes that based commercial cropping on irrigation provided by deep bore wells led to declining ground water tables and the disintegration of traditional water body use that had provided surface water irrigation based on natural stream flows. This situation led to unsustainable resource utilisation systems that did not respect the limiting factor of water in semi-arid environments. More fundamentally, the spread of commercial farming based on horticultural crops led to enclosing of private agricultural lands and their reduced permeability to common usage by way of common grazing. This served to lower the 'adaptive capacity' of the village (cf. Abercrombie et al. 1997) and enhance the risk of accelerated depletion of natural resources in the village, thus increasing its vulnerability to the risks of climate change. The solution is to look at means by which adaptation capabilities of the village can be rendered more robust.

## 2 Trajectory of the Tragedy of Commons in Recent Years

It is noteworthy that a large amount of common grazing lands of the village was converted into reserved forests (345 acres of a total of 545 acres of common grazing lands) in the year 1966, to green the degraded commons. The official machinery considered Mundur's grazing lands use, with its scattered trees and large chunks of grasslands, as unproductive and desired to re-stock the acquired lands with tree plantations. In the 1970s, the common lands that were taken over as reserved forests were planted with *Eucalyptus tereticornis*, a tree which had zero fodder value and poor fuel-wood quality. The only utility of the eucalyptus species was as pulpwood that catered to the raw material needs of the paper and pulpwood industry.

Dense plantations of *Eucalyptus tereticornis* replaced the local silvopastoral land use pattern that was in existence in these lands in the 1960s. The fodder base of Mundur narrowed as a result, resulting in the breakdown of the grazing cycle that was central to the sustainable pattern of natural resources management that existed in the village (cf. Damodaran 2001). Current estimates place the community lands of the village at less than 10% of its total geographical area.

The urban sprawl of Bangalore city had moved dangerously close to Mundur village by the year 2000, aided by the fact that, by the late 1990s, the city had emerged as the "Silicon Valley of Emergent India". The conspicuous consumption patterns noticed amongst the affluent rich and middle class of the city (cf. Damodaran/Haldar 2015) resulted in two trends:

(a) The quest on the part of the new elite to occupy peri-urban spaces of the city for habitation and gentrification;
(b) increasing pressure exerted by Bangalore's urban bureaucracy to convert common waste lands in nearby villages into solid waste dumping yards and landfills to store the large volume of urban wastes being generated by the city.

With its large geographical area and relatively high proportion of degraded common lands, Mundur was one of the ideal candidates for being urban Bangalore's landfill. Thus in the late 1990s urban solid waste from Bangalore found its way to a portion of Mundur's commons, which was in legal possession of the State Forest Department as Reserved Forests. This resulted in grave contamination of the ground water sources of the village due to leachates from the solid waste dump site in the village. Villagers protested against the developments to such an extent that in the year 2015 the State Government ordered the end of solid waste dumping in the village.

# 3 Adaptation Measures

Adaptation measures vary with the source of their action. Adaptation measures can be categorized into two types, "natural" (or "autonomous") and "planned" (cf. Damodaran 2012). While the former involves a natural adjustment process to short lived variability in climate factors, the latter involves conscious interventions on a larger scale to address "secular" changes in climate (cf. Damodaran 2012). Adaptation measures also vary in their source. Thus Robert Mendelsohn categorizes adaptation measures into "public", "private" and "joint" depending upon the agent/agents undertaking adaptation activities and/or receiving its benefits (cf. Mendelsohn 2000). Adaptation is "private" if the decision maker is the only executer and the sole beneficiary of adaptation action. "Joint adaptation", on the other hand, is a group activity whereby action taken by an agent involved affects the benefits other individuals receive. "Public adaptation" occurs when governments invest public financial resources on adaptation activities.

The evidence from Mundur points to the importance of reclaiming the commons from commercialization trends and the adoption of policy solutions that link adaptation-friendly agriculture with traditional knowledge based on CPR-PPR synergies. Thus policies that emphasize food and nutritional self-sufficiency, if coupled with climate action plans that seek to enforce the symbiotic nexus of PPR and CPRs can go a long way in ensuring that sustainable development fits well with the task of increasing the availability of food and nutrients to the peri-urban poor.

# 4 Enhancing Adaptation Capabilities in the Village

The chief lesson that can be gleaned from the traditional resource management systems in the village practised until the 1980s (prior to the advent of bore wells), has been on the importance of utilising private property resources in tandem with common property resources. This means observing and maintaining the delicate balance in traditional man-livestock relations that was based on energy, manure and protein linkages (cf. Damodaran 2001).

It is conceded that the symbiotic state of ecosystem management did not free the village from the scourge of poverty. Landless labourers, particularly groups of which depended exclusively on dry-land agricultural operations for their employment opportunities, were vulnerable to food scarcities during the off-cultivation seasons. However, the symbiotic mode of resource management created conditions for providing a diversified consumption base (comprising of legumes and cereals) to the marginal sections of the village community which in turn helped them to meet the livelihood requirements of landless labourers and small-scale, marginal farmers on a sustainable basis (cf. Damodaran 2001). Today, the marginal farmers in the village who practised dry-land agriculture in the past, have reduced access to quality natural resources (including access to potable water). Since financial institutions provide credit and loans on the basis of collateral instruments such as land titles and also on the basis of likely market rates of return from activities for which loans are sought, it is difficult for traditional vocations and systems of resource management to find support from these institutions.

# 5 The Blueprint for Reclaiming the Commons

Community structures, institutional arrangements, technological interventions, and public policies are considered critical factors that determine the process and condition by which human communities adapt to climate change (cf. Downing et al. 1997). Brian Hurd, Mac Callaway, Joel B. Smith, and Paul Kirshen highlight the importance of market and non-market adaptation measures in the estimation of impact costs (cf. Hurd et al. 1997). Damodaran notes the absence of financing measures for high-end adaptation measures such as artificial recharge of depleted aquifers and evolution of low transpiration plant varieties that could have helped farmers in peri-urban villages of semi-arid India cope with climate stress (cf. Damodaran 2015). The unsustainable situation created by urban sprawl on rural peripheries in developing countries has been highlighted as one of the challenges towards attaining the ideal of inclusive and sustainable cities (cf. Damodaran/Haldar 2015).

Given the patterns described above, the following measures are proposed for reclaiming the commons in terms of their quality and contribution to enhanced adaptation capabilities. Five steps are important to address this issue:

- The *starting point* for reclaiming the commons in the village is to re-vest property rights over common lands and water sources with the village community and its economically weak sectors both by way of legal rights to ownership and 'possession' rights over dry-lands and traditional common property resources including grazing lands and wetlands.
- The *second step* requires a massive effort to clean up the polluted water streams and aquifers.
- The *third step* is to undertake participative hazard analysis and societal risk assessment systems that reflect the local community's perception of the pollution problems facing the village, rather than a solution that is techno-managerial and top-down in approach and looks towards centralized and uniform technical solutions to pollution and other related sustainability problems faced by villages.
- The *fourth step* is to have participative resource mapping. No programme of eco-restoration of village ecosystems can be sustainable unless it is inclusive and par-

ticipative in nature. Villagers also need to be involved in natural resources accounting systems that recognize the ecosystem services rendered by different elements of the village ecosystem. This element normally escapes the attention of centralized resource categorisation and mapping systems. A case in point is the propensity of centralized resource mapping systems to focus on large water bodies and groves, and ignore ecosystem benefits and services provided by small ponds and isolated patches of trees. Only in the event of "minor ecosystem services" being recognised by resource mapping systems would valuation of resources be objective, and sustainable development plans be of relevance to local communities. Thus centralized systems which focus on large and obvious elements and ignore "small" but significant factors that are critical to the livelihood needs of the local communities, need to be given up in favour of local community resource mapping and survey systems.

– The *fifth step* is to ensure flow of finances as it is critical for reclaiming the commons of the village. The traditional system of governmental grants for development activities in the village has proved to be inadequate to the real needs of the village. Local self-government needs to have dedicated financial resources to undertake eco-restoration works and establish management systems to conserve resources. The need is for capital resources to undertake the mammoth tasks of resource rehabilitation. This can be achieved by floating debt instruments like local community "bonds" that can be subscribed to by members of the public. These bonds can be issued on the strength of the monetary value of ecosystem services identified by the community resource mapping systems. If further underwritten by the State, the same bonds would augment flow of capital resources to the village. This will render the task of reclaiming the commons realistic and robust.

To summarize, peri-urban villages which are threatened by urban sprawl reflect one of the greatest threats to ensuring inclusive, sustainable cities in countries like India. These villages which were blessed with commons are threatened by the growing demand from the urban core to open them up for dumping of solid wastes emanating from the city and other top-down actions. Indeed the disappearance of the commons is accompanied by a decline in adaptation capacities, increased hazards to humans and livestock, and grave societal risks. Actions to restore rights over common resources to communities, adoption of clean up measures to eliminate contaminated sites, coupled with hazard analysis, and participative mapping of resources and ecosystem services, will go a long way to achieving the goal of reclaiming the peri-urban commons and enhancing the adaptation capabilities of peri-urban villages in Bangalore and similarly placed cities of India. Organising appropriate financing and institutional mechanisms that aid the process will offer greater possibilities of attaining these goals within a reasonable time period.

## References

Abercrombie, M.; Hickman, C. J.; Johnson, M. L. (1997): A Dictionary of Biology. Harmondsworth

Damodaran, A. (2015): Structuring Climate Financing for Adaptation Measures. In: Braimoh, A.; Huang, H. Q. (2015): Vulnerability of Land Systems in Asia. Chichester, pp. 297–310

Damodaran, A. (2012): The Economics of Coping Strategies and Financing Adaptation Action in India's Semi-arid ecosystems. In: International Journal of Climate Change Strategies and Management, Vol. 4, Issue 4, pp. 386–403

Damodaran, A. (2001): Towards an Agro Ecosystem Policy for India – Lessons from Two Case Studies. Tata McGraw Hill/New Delhi (Centre for Environment Education)

Damodaran, A. (1993): The Endogenous Management of Semi-Arid Watersheds in Karnataka. In: Journal of Environmental Management, Vol. 38, No. 3 (July), pp. 171–183

Damodaran, A.; Haldar, T. (2015): Towards an Agenda for Sustainable and Inclusive, "Low Carbon" Cities for India, Discussion Paper, GIZ-IIMB International Workshop on "Inclusive Sustainable Cities", IIM Bangalore, 12 April

Downing, T. E.; Ringius, L.; Hulme, M.; Waughray, D. (1997): Adapting to Climate Change in Africa. In: Mitigation and Adaptation Strategies for Global Change, Vol. 2, No. 1, pp. 19–44

Hurd, B.; Callaway, M.; Smith, J. B.; Kirshen, P. (1997): Economic Effects of Climate Change on US Water Resources. In: Mendelsohn, R.; Newman, J. (eds): The Impacts of Climate Change on the US Economy. Cambridge, pp. 133–177

Mendelsohn, R. (2000): Efficient Adaptation to Climate Change. In: Climatic Change, Vol. 45, pp. 583–600

Parry, M. L.; Canziani, O. F.; Palutikof, J. P.; Linden, P. J. van der; Hanson, C. E. (eds.) (2007): Climate Change 2007: Impacts, Adaptation and Vulnerability, Contribution of Working Group II to the Fourth Assessment Report of the Intergovernmental Panel on Climate Change. Cambridge

## 3. Opportunities and Challenges for Sustainable Cities

katja saar

# Co-housing

## Abundant Potential for Sustainable Housing and Neighbourhood Development

*Anja Szypulski*

## 1 Introduction

During the last 30 years the number of co-housing projects in various countries has increased in response to major societal trends. The demographic changes include aging populations, decreasing household sizes, and more diverse family structures, which are reflected by a growing demand for new dwelling types. Co-housing projects offer new qualities of life, and therefore, are growing in relevance for urban development and housing.

Co-housing projects are mainly characterized by a focus on community: "Residents share a vision of community-oriented living" (Id22 2012, p. 17) which is based on community activities, mutual help and a reliable neighbourhood. The residents share common spaces and facilities, making the idea of community visible. Most of the projects are characterized by a cooperative planning and management of the projects, reflecting the growing interest in communication, self-organisation and participation (cf. Mensch 2011; Szypulski 2008).

Due to family structure and demographic changes, co-housing is increasingly appealing to older as well as younger people, for families as well as singles. Co-housing projects attract people that have consciously chosen a mutually supportive and cooperative lifestyle in various degrees. Often, these projects include a mixture of different types of households, income levels, and cultural backgrounds.

A wide range of projects have been developed during the last years. They are organised in different forms: projects for homeowners in building communities, rental projects in cooperation with municipal housing companies, and as traditional and new cooperatives and more market-oriented models realised by housing companies. The projects touch different aspects: ecological building, affordability, different user groups, multigenerational housing, women's projects, intercultural projects, and integrative housing for people with and without disabilities (cf. Id22 2012).

This article examines the potential of co-housing for sustainable housing and neighbourhood development. It also looks at the development of co-housing projects in Germany, discusses the new qualities of housing these projects provide, and identifies obstacles and barriers in the realisation of co-housing projects. Finally, the article discusses the implications for urban housing policy.

## 2 Development of Co-housing Projects in Germany

Motives and objectives of co-housing projects are manifold. The study of Joachim Brech identifies the first co-housing projects in the 1970s as experiments that wanted to change social life and society (cf. Brech 1999). During the 1980s the number of co-housing projects increased and the projects were characterized by an orientation towards special user groups (e.g. single parents, families). Beside the community orientation, many projects also pursued a programmatic objective such as ecological housing. Most of the projects during this period were realised by families as home-owners. For the 1990s Micha Fedrowitz observes an emphasis on projects for the elderly ("not alone and not in a senior home"; cf. Fedrowitz 2010, 2011). Since 2000, many co-housing projects have been following a multigenerational approach.

How many co-housing projects exist in Germany? It is difficult to find an answer to this question but based on present publications a first approach is possible. The ongoing research of Fedrowitz records a total of 501 realised co-housing projects in Germany and about another 100 projects in different stages of planning (cf. Fedrowitz 2011). More than 50% of these projects were realised between 2000 and 2010. Considering the difficulties of this kind of survey it can be assumed that the number of co-housing projects is considerably higher and has increased especially during the last ten years. Fedrowitz also shows regional differences in the spatial distribution of co-housing projects with a concentration in Hamburg, Berlin, Munich and North Rhine-Westphalia (cf. Fedrowitz 2011).

Looking at the legal form of co-housing projects, it can be recognized that during recent years a great variety of organisational structures have emerged (e.g. cooperation with municipal housing companies, traditional and new cooperatives, and building of communities). According to the study of Fedrowitz, about one third of the co-housing projects are organized as cooperatives (cf. Fedrowitz 2011). Housing cooperatives are characterized by self-organisation, self-determination and the principle of solidarity. For many co-housing projects the legal form of a cooperative reflects the idea of community betterment.

In 2011 the Federal Institute for Research on Building, Urban Affairs and Spatial Development started a research project on "multigenerational co-housing projects in the legal form of a registered cooperative". Multigenerational projects are recognized as a sub-category of co-housing projects if at least three generations (children, parents, grandparents who are not necessarily relatives) live together. The research focuses on the relevance of co-housing projects in the form of a cooperative in terms of size, structure and regional distribution. As the legal form of cooperative housing projects varies, three types of cooperatives were defined for the collection and analysis of data: traditional cooperatives, newly established individual cooperatives, and housing projects as part of so-called "roof-cooperatives" (Dachgenossenschaften) (cf. Fedrowitz et al. 2012).

The survey showed an increase in the number of realised projects. In total 131 co-housing projects were found in the legal form of a cooperative (1988-2011). 106 projects were realised in the period from 2000-2011 (2000-2006: 5 to 8 realised projects a year, 2007-2011: 10 to 13 realised projects a year). This confirms the growing interest in co-housing projects during the last ten years, particularly in the period between 2007 and 2011. The majority of projects consist of 21 to 50 housing units and were realised in new buildings. The survey also shows regional differences in the relevance of cooperative projects: main areas are Hamburg (27) and Berlin (11), Hessen (13) and North Rhine-Westphalia (13) (cf. Fedrowitz et al. 2012).

The increasing relevance of living in multigenerational housing is reflected in the high frequency these projects have among the total of cooperative projects, as the survey proves. Between 2000 and 2011, a total of 57 out of 106 projects, which amounts to more than 50%, followed a multigenerational approach. During that period the number of multigenerational projects increased considerably: from 12 projects between 2000 and 2005 to 45 projects between 2006 and 2011 (cf. Fedrowitz et al. 2012).

Considering the current figures and follow-up surveys, a further increase in the number of co-housing projects in all legal forms can be expected in the future, especially those projects with a multigenerational approach. Still, only a small percentage of people are currently living in co-housing projects. The emergence of the co-housing landscape in Germany (and Europe) reflects that co-housing projects are more than a new market segment or a niche, but also an indicator for housing needs that cannot be realised in regular housing types. Regarding urban development, co-housing is currently not of quantitative but of qualitative significance.

## 3 Enhanced Qualities of Housing are Required – Co-housing Projects Provide Answers to Current Questions

Co-housing projects can provide answers to current social problems and future questions, and often offer new qualities of life. These are social, ecological and participatory qualities of planning, building processes, and daily life. Most of the projects represent high ecological standards and high quality architecture. Furthermore, co-housing projects have considerably contributed to the development of a new participative planning culture and a new generation of cooperatives as mentioned before (cf. Behrens/Bura 2002; Breckner 1999; Wohnbund 2013). This article focuses on three aspects: providing housing suitable for the elderly, affordable housing, and the potential of co-housing for neighbourhood development.

## 3.1 Housing Suitable for the Elderly

Due to changes in family structures and demographics, multigenerational housing is increasingly appealing to older as well as younger people. Multigenerational projects provide benefits, especially on the level of everyday help between residents. The elderly and families with children especially benefit from these. Beside multigenerational projects, many co-housing initiatives for the elderly have developed during the last twenty years.

One result of our case studies in the formerly mentioned was that any additional care services, particularly for the elderly, are usually not covered by other residents, but provided by professionals. In the multigenerational project, Muehlbachhaus, the residents report positive experiences with mutual everyday support (e.g. shopping) but being in need of care, the residents work with a mobile care service. If the demand for care grows, the project intends to use one of the housing units for a nurse. (cf. Fedrowitz et al. 2012).

Nevertheless, other investigations show that neighbourly help can postpone a stay in a nursing home. Since multigenerational projects have usually realised barrier-free buildings, they offer good conditions for the elderly, as well as for families with children (cf. Fedrowitz et al. 2012).

The multigenerational project Amaryllis eG and the "sister project" Villa Emma eG in Bonn are excellent examples of the benefits of co-housing for the elderly and for people in need of assistance. Both projects are realised as new cooperatives. After the realisation of Amaryllis; a group of residents decided to work on another project in the same neighbourhood for people in need of assistance. Consequently, Villa Emma eG was founded in 2011. This co-housing project offers eleven barrier-free housing units suitable for wheelchairs, common rooms, and a guest room. 13 residents (22 to 90 years), some of them in need of assistance, live in the project. A 24-hour care service, located in Villa Emma eG,[1] is used by the residents and is also available to the neighbourhood (cf. Fedrowitz et al 2012).

The founders of Villa Emma understand their project as a civil initiative of the neighbourhood. The engagement of the residents of the neighbourhood is an important

1 Cf. www.villa-emma-bonn.de.

element of daily life in the project. This initiative can also be seen as a support for the elderly in the Amaryllis project in case they are in need of special care. Another important aspect was to develop a care service point in the neighbourhood (cf. Fedrowitz et al. 2012[2]).

## 3.2 Provision of Affordable Housing

In view of social polarisation, gentrification processes, and rising rents in the cities, many initiatives are placing value on the provision of affordable housing in the form of rental projects or cooperatives. Furthermore, the combination of private ownership and rental units owned by investors, housing companies, and cooperatives enable social mixes within a co-housing project. But to provide affordable housing, many projects are dependent on funding. Cooperative ownership structures offer a non-profit compromise between renting and owning. In newly-built cooperatives the realization of co-housing projects requires a sustainable amount of equity of each member. Therefore, problems of financing are often mentioned as obstacles for the foundation of a cooperative (cf. Wohnbund 2013).

In some of the co-housing projects, the idea of community leads to an internal solidarity concerning the financial aspects. In the case studies we found elements of solidarity-based financing in two projects: Amaryllis (Bonn) and Muehlbachhaus (Schorndorf). Both projects established a fund to help the residents who could not afford the compulsory contribution of capital for the cooperative. The cooperative signed a non-interest loan agreement with the residents concerned (cf. Fedrowitz et al. 2012).

Additionally, some of the projects find new solutions to enable social mixes. In Schorndorf, individual homeownership is combined with cooperative rental units. The greater financial resources of the homeowners were partly used to enhance the ecological standard of the project and were an indispensable prerequisite for the realisation of this project (cf. Fedrowitz et al. 2012).

## 3.3 Development of Neighbourhoods

In recent years, the positive effects of co-housing have also been discussed in the context of social urban development. Active political efforts are subjects of these discussions, as well as the more implicit social and cultural contributions of co-housing to urban development. Co-housing projects not only affect the living and housing situations of the residents, but also influence the surrounding neighbourhoods (cf. Behrens/Bura 2002; Id22 2012).

2 Cf. www.villa-emma-bonn.de too.

Many co-housing projects interact with surrounding neighbourhoods and demonstrate the potential for sustainable neighbourhoods instead of social exclusion (cf. Szypulski 2008, p. 56). They provide infrastructure, and share common facilities with the residents of the neighbourhood. Co-housing projects can be seen as reliable partners in urban development processes, and as an important element of a forward-looking strategy for neighbourhood development. Moreover, due to the engagement of the residents of the projects, self-organisation and self-help for neighbourhood development can often be assumed (cf. Id22 2012; Wohnbund 2013).

# 4 Barriers and Their Implications for Housing Policies

During the last years, a variety of support structures for co-housing projects have been developed, often by housing policy actors (e.g. Wohnbund e.V., Forum Gemeinschaftliches Wohnen) and municipalities. These initiatives are focused on information and networking. Moreover, a professional network of engaged experts has emerged and a couple of cities have established strategies and instruments to support co-housing (e.g. Hamburg, Munich and Frankfurt) (cf. Schuetter 2010). Positioning for further projects has thus been improved, especially in the field of information and the establishment of contacts though barriers still exist.

## 4.1 Support by Local Authorities

The activities of municipalities in the field of co-housing take various forms. Some are developing first approaches; other municipalities establish advice centres for co-housing projects (e.g. Dortmund, Frankfurt am Main). These can be seen as basic conditions to promote co-housing. Project initiatives and developers as well as investors are provided with information, and a network between groups, other relevant stakeholders and competent authorities is initiated.

Cities like Freiburg and Tuebingen have adopted co-housing as a main principle of their land allocation and as an essential element of urban development strategies (cf. Kraemer/Kuhn 2009). But apart from these exceptions, systematic municipal support of co-housing projects is only weakly developed. A lack of support during project conceptualization is often reported from co-housing projects (cf. Fedrowitz et al. 2012).

The willingness of institutions, especially banks and local authorities, to support co-housing projects often emerges only *after* a successful realisation (cf. Fedrowitz et al. 2012). Many projects therefore have to develop complex financial concepts including funding and elements of solidarity-based financing. Apart from a few exceptions, the housing sector has not been very engaged in co-housing until now.

## 4.2 Funding

In the initial phase of project development, the financial risks for the initiators are particularly high. Small amounts of financial support at this stage are highly efficient in encouraging the group. Assistance during the early phases of the project with small funding can enable the formation of stable groups. In Germany, there are few funding opportunities that include the promotion of project development. Some federal states also support the establishment of common spaces as part of social housing programs (e.g. Hamburg, North-Rhine Westphalia) (cf. Berghaeuser 2008; Fedrowitz et al. 2012).

Referring cooperative co-housing projects, promotion of social housing should be available for cooperatives in all federal states. The promotion of newly established cooperatives can contribute to a social mixture and an inter-generational focus on co-housing and neighbourhoods. Furthermore, loans from banks ought to be available for newly established cooperatives and be secured by state guarantees, if necessary (cf. Fedrowitz et al. 2012).

## 4.3 Access to Land

Research on co-housing shows that availability of land is the main barrier when developing a new co-housing project. Due to the specific development process and timing, it is usually not possible for co-housing initiatives to acquire land within the usual tender period. The allocation of plots normally depends on the price. This procedure neglects the social, ecological, and democratic qualities of co-housing projects. Support by local authorities in identifying plots of land or existing buildings is therefore considered to be particularly important. The reservation of plots for co-housing projects during the phase of conceptualization or subsidized supply of land would be of great help. As mentioned before, some cities have adopted co-housing as a main principle of their land allocation – but what about implementation in a background of market-oriented competition where investors possess much more financial (and political) resources?

# 5 Conclusion

While the experiences of co-housing projects have already been well documented in different publications (cf. Ginski et al. 2012; Id22 2012; McCamant/Durrett 1989; Vestbro 2010; Wohnbund 2013), there is a lack of research in this field. co-housing is a transdisciplinary field of study that addresses complex issues of sustainable urban development, housing policy, and questions of civil society and engagement.

The last decade has shown the great diversity of co-housing initiatives and how they address important issues. Despite existing studies of co-housing we still know very little about the motives and expectations of the residents; how they change over the years; how to organize the management of a project after realisation; and how co-housing projects contribute to their surroundings. Though studies have been published on local strategies, there is no systematic overview of local strategies and instruments that have been implemented to tackle this issue. It would also be beneficial to learn from other European countries and establish systematic networks to link fragmented national knowledge and experiences.

Contemporary debates show a rising awareness that some cities in Germany have to deal with privatisation and gentrification processes, as well as rising rents, leading to the challenge of providing affordable housing. As we have seen, co-housing initiatives make substantial contributions to innovative housing with regard to attractive architecture, ecological and social qualities, and affordability. But, "co-housing groups are often overpowered by market forces and housing policies" (Id22 2012, p. 31). To foster innovative approaches, a commitment to residents, and social responsibility in the provision of affordable housing, we need to (re)establish a non-profit housing sector.

## References

Behrens, T.; Bura, J. (2002): Neue Wohnungsbaugenossenschaften in Hamburg. In: Stattbau Hamburg (ed.): Wohnprojekte, Baugemeinschaften, Soziale Stadtentwicklung. Das Stattbaubuch. Hamburg, pp. 20–24 (in German)

Berghaeuser, M. (2008): Wie Bayern, Berlin, Hamburg und Co. gemeinschaftliches Wohnen fördern. In: Schader-Stiftung; Stiftung Trias (eds.): Raus aus der Nische – rein in den Markt! Herten, pp. 95–108 (in German)

Brech, J. (1999): Ein Wandel im Wohnen in der Zeit des Umbruchs. Eine Studie zu Neuen Wohnformen. In: Wüstenrot-Stiftung (ed.): Neue Wohnformen im internationalen Vergleich. Stuttgart a.o., pp. 81–160 (in German)

Breckner, I. (1999): Wohnprojekte. Luxus für wenige oder gesellschaftlicher Bedarf? In: Info für gemeinschaftliches und selbstbestimmtes Wohnen, Vol. 4, pp. 1–2 (in German)

Fedrowitz, M. (2010): Gemeinschaft in der Stadt. Das Modell des Mehrgenerationenwohnens. In: Informationskreis für Raumplanung e.V. (2010). RaumPlanung, Heft 149. Dortmund, pp. 75–80 (in German)

Fedrowitz, M. (2011): Gemeinschaftliches Wohnen in Deutschland. In: Nationalatlas aktuell 9 (09/2011). Leipzig (IfL – Leibniz-Institut für Länderkunde). – URL: http://aktuell.nationalatlas.de/Gemeinschaftliches_Wohnen.9_09-2011.0.html (in German)

Fedrowitz, M.; Kiehle, W.; Szypulski, A. (2012): Mehrgenerationen-Wohnprojekte in der Rechtsform der eingetragenen Genossenschaft eG. BBSR Forschungsvorhaben. Unveröffentlichter Abschlussbericht. Bochum. Short Version. – URL: http://www.bbsr.bund.de/BBSR/DE/FP/ReFo/Wohnungswesen/2011/MehrgenerationenWohnen/01_Start.html?nn=439538&notFirst=false (in German)

Ginski, S.; Koller, B.; Schmitt, G. (2012): IBA Berlin 2020. Besondere Wohnformen. Auftraggeber: Senatsverwaltung für Stadtentwicklung und Umwelt Berlin. Aachen. – URL: http://www.stadtentwicklung.berlin.de/staedtebau/baukultur/iba/de/studien.shtml (in German)

Kraemer, S.; Kuhn, G. (2009): Städte und Baugemeinschaften. Stuttgart a.o. (in German)

Id22 – Institute for Creative Sustainability: Experimentcity (2012): CO Housing Cultures. Handbook for Self-organized, Community-oriented and Sustainable Housing. Berlin

McCamant, K.; Durrett, C. (1989): Cohousing. A Contemporary Approach to Housing Ourselves. Berkeley

Mensch, K. (2011): Gemeinschaftliches Wohnen – der Versuch einer Definition. In: Wohnbund e.V. (ed.): Perspektiven für Wohnprojekte. München, pp 8–11 (wohnbund-informationen, 01/2011) (in German)

Schader-Stiftung; Stiftung Trias (eds.) (2008): Raus aus der Nische – rein in den Markt! Herten (in German)

Schuetter, J. B. (2010): Handlungsmöglichkeiten und –notwendigkeiten von Kommunen im Umgang mit Wohnprojekten. Diplomarbeit. Dortmund (Technische Universität Dortmund) (in German)

Stattbau Hamburg (2002) (ed.): Wohnprojekte Baugemeinschaften Soziale Stadtentwicklung. Das Stattbau-Buch. Hamburg (in German)

Szypulski, A. (2008): Gemeinsam bauen – gemeinsam wohnen. Wohneigentumsbildung durch Selbsthilfe. Wiesbaden (in German)

Vestbro, D. U. (2010): Living Together – Cohousing Ideas and Realities around the World. Stockholm

Wohnbund e.V. (ed.) (2013): Wir wohnen anders! Neue Wohnungsgenossenschaften gestalten Lebensräume und finden dabei Antworten auf gesellschaftliche Zukunftsfragen. Hannover (in German)

# Gender & Diversity

## Issues and Challenges for the "Just City"

*Sandra Huning*

## 1 Introduction

This paper aims to address issues and challenges that arise when gender relations and diversity are considered in sustainable and just urban and neighbourhood development policies. Cities and neighbourhoods can be built and organized to become resources for different social groups and lifestyles, but they can also set limits for others. Gender, class (income, education), ethnicity, and other categories of social differentiation have an important impact on the ways that urban spaces are appropriated, used, and shaped. The transformation of gender and other social relations over the last decades has led to new spatial demands. This paper argues that understanding both these transformations and the ways they have been reflected in urban development strategies is an important precondition for promoting sustainable and just urban development.

The paper starts by discussing the path of gender and diversity issues into urban development. Afterwards, it discusses what justice may mean when it comes to the acknowledgement of these issues in urban planning and development. Justice is a normative concept and its definition not uncontested. Thereforethere are not precise technical answers, but rather an adaptable framework for policies that strive for just and sustainable urban development.

## 2 From Feminist Interventions to Gender Mainstreaming in Urban Development

In recent urban studies and politics, diversity issues get much more attention than gender relations - for several reasons. One argument for the use of diversity instead of gender concepts is that gender is automatically part of and has been integrated into diversity politics. Another argument, frequently disguised as "common sense" in spite of its obvious ignorance of facts and figures, is that gender equality has made so much progress over the past decades that a specific focus on this particular category of social differentiation can no longer be justified (cf. Greed 2005). The different "careers" of the concepts of gender and diversity are actually quite revealing in terms of which perspectives are recognised as legitimate and which are not, and they give different insights for the idea of just urban development.

Feminist research in urban sociology and urban planning started in the 1970s (cf. Dörhöfer/Terlinden 1998; contributions in Fainstein/Servon 2005a; Fainstein/Servon 2005b; Roberts 2013) and emerged from the second women's movement which claimed that women's socio-spatial needs were neglected in patriarchal post-war societies and had to be considered more thoroughly in architecture and planning. From then on, feminist architects and planners researched the needs of women and the ways women appropriated space, and analysed how spatial structures made women's everyday routines difficult. Based on this research, they suggested how planning could become more sensitive to women's needs.

One key issue from the very beginning was the functional division of urban space. For example, in the rapidly growing late 19th/early 20th century modernising cities in Germany, under the conditions of early capitalist development and industrialisation, women not only had the chance to gain an independent income in new industrial or office jobs, but they also experienced new liberties in the appropriation of public spaces (cf. von Saldern 2004; Wilson 1991). Working women, however, were considered a threat to the moral health of the working class in general and the family in particular by the bourgeois upper classes. Therefore, the subsequent functional division of urban spaces and the process of suburbanisation were inspired not only by requirements of capitalist production, but also by the desire to re-establish gender orders and to locate women and the whole sphere of reproductive work in the safe environments of suburbia (cf. Frank 2008) – not only in Germany, but also in the United States (cf. Hayden 2002; 2005; Markusen 1991). These environments provided housing for the individual household of the nuclear family, but only rarely did they also offer local retail and other services, leisure facilities, adequate public transportation, or any job opportunities for women. Evidently, they established and reproduced a dominant gender order of a male breadwinner and a female housewife.

In West Germany, this gender order was reflected in post-war social housing in a particular layout of the housing unit, but also of the housing estate as a whole (cf. Dörhöfer/Terlinden 1998). Funding schemes prescribed clearly defined apartment sizes and standardised norms for the apartment layout. The Frankfurt kitchen which had been development by Viennese architect Margarete Schütte-Lohatzky in the 1920s in accordance with workflow studies by the American Christine Frederick is one example of the rationalization of housework. It made work in the kitchen easier in certain regards compared to earlier, less practically equipped kitchens, but it prevented an equal share of household tasks among household members and the combination of kitchen and care work. Furthermore, the standardised apartment layout of social housing was criticized by the second women's movement for not taking into account alternative household types such as one-parent families whose spatial needs and financial resources differed from the nuclear family so that they had no chance to qualify for social housing (cf. Becker 1992).

The public-private divide which was represented in the functional division of space both in the apartment and in residential urban areas was also criticized in more general terms. First of all, it stipulated the gendered division of labour and the ideals of "public man" and "private woman", and it relegated reproductive work to the private sphere without taking into account political "public" responsibility. Secondly, the division contributed to the common perception that public spaces were considered inappropriate and unsafe for virtuous women, and this notion continued to be reproduced in spite of all statistics showing that assaults on women were generally located in private rather than in public spaces. In the use of open spaces, gendered ways to use and appropriate space could be observed (cf. Huning 2012).

Based on this knowledge, the transformation of housing and settlement patterns over time can be better understood. Suburban single family housing has until today been the spatial symbol for the ideal type of modern housing: living together in a nuclear family in accordance with the breadwinner-housewife-model. This model still exists, but it is no longer prevalent which can be attributed to the diversification of gender roles for women and consequently to changed gender relations. The number of children per family has decreased, and household types and lifestyles have multiplied to: DINK (double income no kids), LAT (living apart together), or YUP (young urban professional) households. Suburban areas have lost their appeal and other settlement patterns have become much more attractive. The demand for housing has changed, and central inner-city locations have become much more attractive for these new household types, because, among other factors, the accessibility of urban functions has become a more important location factor. Changing gender roles for women (and partly for their children and/or for men) were found to have a considerable impact on gentrification processes (cf. Berg 2014; Bondi 1991; 1995).

Feminist architects and planners suggested ways to overcome the spatial manifestation of traditional gender orders and the gendered division of labour by designing spaces either with a particular focus on women's needs, with a stronger user-orientation in general, or with a focus on overcoming structural barriers (cf. Hayden 2005). In the late 1990s, the concept of gender mainstreaming entered the feminist discourse in a situation where the limits of the strategies that had been employed became visible (cf. Becker 1998; Dörhöfer/Terlinden 1998; Rodenstein 1998). Feminist claims had until then been integrated into the planning mainstream to an extent that their feminist origin had become more or less invisible, and paradoxically the successes of the second women's movement made the specific consideration of women's needs to appear less urgent. But in spite of this early type of "mainstreaming", equity had still not been reached. The heterogeneity of women's needs was increasingly recognized so that it seemed no longer possible to speak of women as one collective subject. This made it much harder to draft powerful claims. In this situation, gender mainstreaming promised a new approach with a strong formal top-down commitment. In planning it was welcomed by many as a promising approach to tackle gender inequalities (cf. Bauhardt 2003; Roberts 2013).

In the meantime, this optimism has partly faded (cf. Caglar 2013). One key objection towards gender mainstreaming approaches has been that it is not, or not adequately, taking up feminist's critical stance towards power relations and domination and might even stabilize traditional gender orders. Gender mainstreaming as a political approach has not always been clear in what it aims to achieve. The equal consideration of men's and women's needs does not automatically lead to an overcoming of the two-sex binary which has been criticized by gender and homosexual studies for quite some time (cf. Hark 2001). Critics fear that the social construction of sex and gender is not always adequately addressed. There are, however, gender mainstreaming strategies which explicitly aim to address these criticisms (cf. Greed 2005). At this point, it seems that there are many discourses on gender planning which are more or less linked to each other. A single commonly recognized and accepted approach does not exist (cf. Huning 2013).

# 3 Managing Diversity in Urban Development

In comparison with the gender discourse, the concept of urban diversity has come into focus of urban research only recently, although, social differentiation and social inequality in cities have been key topics in urban sociology ever since the Chicago School. Urban inequalities were tackled by much research which aimed to inform urban planning and development to fight poverty and urban decline. The recognition of the social and cultural differentiation of cities' populations increased over the last two decades (cf. Sandercock 2003; Waltz 2014) so that the need to deal with "diversity" came up in cities in the U.S. and Canada, but also in Europe and Germany. Diversity management is not yet a common tool in urban development but it is, at least in many German cities, particularly employed to deal with the integration of population groups of different ethnic backgrounds. Although in theory, diversity can refer to many other categories of social differentiation and is seen as "potential" for urban development, in urban politics it refers mainly to "new paths for integration" (cf. Bohle et al. 2004; Schuster 2014).

Diversity management was developed for businesses with reference to their heterogeneous staff and their diverse clients (cf. Vedder 2006). It was seen as a tool to improve a company's economic performance because barriers due to different cultures, genders, and other social categories were supposed to be dismantled and addressed, while at the same time new clients were supposed to be reached through more inclusive and diversity-sensitive production and marketing. This economic argument was also prevalent in the further dissemination of "diversity" in urban policies. The ideal of the "creative city" promoted by urbanists such as Richard Florida, Charles Landry, and others, made population diversity a desirable urban feature (cf. Florida 2005; Landry 2000). These authors argued that urban diversity and a high degree of mutual tolerance for different lifestyles provide an inspiring environment for the so-called "creative" middle classes whom they found to be important for economic growth in today's urban economies. In this view, diversity is a location factor for economic development in an increasingly competitive urban system under the influence of globalization, inter- and transnationalisation (cf. Smith 2000).

Diversity in practice has been employed in a variety of ways. In Germany, it has inspired integration policies in cities such as Frankfurt/Main, Hamburg and Göttingen (cf. Bohle et al. 2004). While the German chancellor Angela Merkel claims that "multiculturalism has utterly failed" (Sueddeutsche Zeitung, 16 October 2010), diversity politics is based on the new hope that social and cultural differentiation of the population must not be seen as a problem to be solved, but can actually be a benefit for urban societies. "The diversity politics concept offers cities the opportunity for an individual and flexible reaction to change. It is detached from typical fields of action and rather describes a working and action principle for the municipal administration... Diversity politics presents a theoretical framework for cities which they can fill and employ according to their needs" (Bohle et al. 2004, p. 203; translated by the author). This quote reflects the openness of the concept which has also affected debates on affordable housing, social mixing, and residential de-segregation (cf. Blokland/Eijk 2010). In this context, it has been argued that cross-cultural communication is a critical competence for planners in today's diverse societies. Some authors define it as a specific mode of thinking and a kind of self-reflection of a planner's own everyday work (cf. Agyeman/Erickson 2012; Reeves 2011).

The definition of diversity and the question of which categories of differentiation actually constitute it (ethnicity, gender, age, sexual orientation, etc.) is not self-evident. Any definition bears the risk of essentialism when characteristics are attributed to specific groups without taking into account the social construction of these attributes (cf. Schuster 2014). Here we can see a parallel to some gender debates explicitly referring to men and women. Debates on diversity also tend to highlight the potential gains of a diverse population without taking into account strategies to overcome social inequalities, which in many regards cause expressions of diversity in the first place. Critics plead to bear in mind that diversity (just as gender) is not "natural", but that it is a consequence of differentiation processes, and it is therefore not banal to analyse power relations and forms of domination which determine whether a category is considered as relevant or not.

What follows from such diversity goals for urban politics? "The decisive question is how a city can be designed materially and symbolically, socially and spatially so that all residents have the most possible opportunities and chances for self-fulfilment" (Frank 2004, p. 212), no matter what their gender, sexual orientation, cultural/ethnic background, or age may be. This is a goal which is hard to reach, in particular in inner cities which have become more attractive recently because of the above-mentioned transformation of gender relations and the increasing recognition of diversity as potential for a creative urban environment. Affordable housing is one challenge which derives from the new focus on inner cities, as are climate change mitigation and adaptation strategies for more sustainable development. As a consequence, the question of justice (not only) in the transformation of inner cities is an important one. It may be a coincidence (or not) that planning theorists re-entered the debate on the "Just City" only a few years ago (cf. Fainstein 2010).

## 4 The Just City and Just Diversity

Several planning theoretical models have addressed the question of how social differentiation and social inequality can be better taken into account in planning processes. In the 1960s, Paul Davidoff's advocacy planning model aimed for a better representation of minorities and low-income households in planning processes (cf. Davidoff 1965). The model raised attention to deprived groups and made planners' norms and values more transparent. The question of redistribution was addressed by the equity planning model of Norman Krumholz and John Forester (cf. Krumholz/Forester 1990) who stressed the responsibility of planners to "speak truth to power" and to present planning outcomes which contributed to equity (recently also discussed by Susan Fainstein with reference to the "just city"; cf. Fainstein 2005). Patsy Healey focused on fair shares of different stakeholders in collaborative planning processes and argued for a communicative rationality which recognizes differences: "We see things differently because words, phrases, expressions, objects, are interpreted differently according to our frame of reference. It is this point [...] which underpins the strength of the relativist position" (Healey 1992, p. 152). Theoretical approaches which understand planning as "persuasive storytelling" (cf. Throgmorton 2003) stress the importance of giving room to different, competing stories from a variety of stakeholders to reflect the complexity of social relations. In this perspective, it is important to create as many opportunities as possible for a variety of storytellers and stories (cf. Sandercock 2000; 2003). Many theories take a social constructivist view when they highlight that social realities do not exist outside social relations, but that they are constituted in the context of stakeholders' relative positions, identifications, interpretations, and resources.

But what would a just city be like? This question is particularly difficult to answer since the definition of justice in socio-spatial terms is by no means self-evident. Most cities are characterised by diversity and inequality – in terms of settlement and building structures, socio-spatial, and socio-economic functions, but also in the distribution of different social and demographic groups throughout urban space as they are reflected in debates on segregation, polarization, and de-mixing (cf. Bridge et al. 2012). These inequalities are not always interpreted as injustice. Rather, justice depends on the respective context, is a rather relative concept, and also has to do with who is actually able in a certain situation to enforce a certain definition of justice. When the Greek Thrasymachos told Sokrates that what is just is what is beneficial for the strongest, he raised attention to power relations which coin understandings of justice and the way these are institutionalised.

Harvard professor Susan Fainstein, a key protagonist in current just city debates, has argued (with reference to Martha Nussbaum) that justice relates to equity, equity being defined as the proactive ensuring of certain indisputable capabilities which everyone should be entitled to. These capabilities may comprise life itself, to make a living, health, bodily integrity, access to education, and influence on one's own political and material environment. To ensure urban justice and the "right to the city" (Lefebvre) for each individual urban resident is for Fainstein a key aim of urban politics and planning, and independent of higher goals and any kind of common welfare. Fainstein certainly acknowledges conflicts of interest in capitalist societies. To reach equity in the sense of a positive action, established democratic procedures are not enough and planners need to pay special attention to ensure minorities' rights in the political process.

The recent financial crisis and changes in the global environmental pose quite difficult conditions for the realisation of equity planning and politics. If natural resources become scarce, who will be able to develop coping strategies will depend highly on financial resources. Rising energy costs may make cars, heating and electric devices unaffordable for poor households so that their "right to the city" may be affected. As long as resources are distributed along social categories such as gender and ethnicity, current crises affect social groups in different ways, but there may be contradictory goals and interests which make it difficult to realize key capabilities for all. The Australian planners Ruth Fincher and Kurt Iveson introduced the term "just diversity", hoping this might lead planners to reflect their role in the reproduction of urban inequality and make their normative standpoints more transparent: "If planning is to craft more just cities in a context of diversity, then this cannot be simply a matter of accommodating or embracing diversity as such. Rather, it is a matter of disentangling the different kinds of diversity which characterize city life and distinguishing between those forms of diversity which are just and those that are unjust" (Fincher/Iveson 2008, p. 3).

In contrast to diversity management in the narrower sense, "just diversity" is broader in that it means that planners should consider three interrelated social logics: "redistribution, through which attempts are made to plan for the redress of disadvantage; recognition, through which efforts are made to define the attributes of groups of people so that their needs can be met; and encounter, through which the interaction of individuals is planned in order to offer opportunities for increased sociality" (Fincher/Iveson 2008, p. 3). This inclusive perspective is based on feminist and diversity claims and not only addresses the needs of different population groups, but also the mechanisms through which they are reproduced.

# 5 The Role of Participation

"The role of planners in facilitating the participation of these different groups of citizens in matters of urban policy has become a key concern for planning scholarship and practice" (Fincher/Iveson 2008, p. 3). Participation is a key element in gender and diversity discourses, but it is as such not considered sufficient to promote just diversity by those authors who are interested in just urban development. The focus on the "communicative turn" in planning ever since the 1990s oriented towards the procedures of urban planning and put less emphasis on substantial outcomes. Although for planners it is still common sense that participation improves the results of a planning process, not to speak of its legitimacy; the danger of selective participation and of the reproduction of power inequalities prevails, no matter how well-intended the participation processes might be (cf. Huning 2014). Lately, authors introducing the concepts of post-politics or post-democracy (cf. Crouch 2008; Wagner 2013) have claimed that participation is very frequently employed as a means to stabilize power relations and not to change them.

Fincher and Iveson therefore argue: "to create more just cities, planners need a framework for *making judgements between* different claims in the planning process, as well as for *facilitating* them" (Fincher/Iveson 2008, original emphasis). They argue that planners still tend to see themselves as neutral experts who are able to act in some kind of common interest instead of understanding their role in political terms, and suggest that this may not do justice to today's complex governance systems. Participation must then employ a broad range of methods not only to make different voices heard, but to actually elaborate which needs and conflicts lie behind the stories that are told. In order to make participation strategies in particular and urban development more integrative, some urban researchers are in favour of participation strategies which do not only consist of traditional procedures of discourse and verbal exchange, but include opportunities of spatial appropriation. The Dutch environmentalists Esther Turnhout, Severine Van Bommel, and Noelle Aarts understand participation as performative practice where identities, knowledge, interests, and needs are not represented, but shaped and articulated (cf. Turnhout et al. 2010). They aim to overcome essentialist identifications of target groups with special needs, and to offer different arenas for action and partaking in urban development. One prerequisite, however, for a successful exchange is in any case the openness and transparency of the process; if the scope of decision-making is too limited, the results may be discouraging instead of enhancing (cf. Bernt/Fritsche 2008).

The "just diversity" discourse argues that participation does not necessarily lead to more "just" planning outcomes. In many cases, it may mean no more than private interests (legitimate or illegitimate) trying to make their point to the disadvantage of others who remain silent. Accordingly, participation does not replace structural compensation such as affordable housing policies. However, to open up opportunities participation may help to develop visions for new forms of sharing spaces in cities and for cooperation, important prerequisites for sustainable urban development.

# 6 Conclusion

This paper addressed a few of the issues and challenges that arise when gender and diversity are taken into account in the context of just and sustainable urban development. Early feminist approaches stressed the need for positivist action in favour of women whose socio-spatial needs had been neglected or subsumed under the one-dimensional role of a housewife; i.e. in favour of one collective subject or target group. When it became more difficult to argue for women collectively, gender mainstreaming opened the discussion beyond women to include all genders. But this is difficult to implement. Some gender policies are based on essentialist gender definitions and contribute to a stabilization of gender roles instead of their dissolution. This danger is also apparent when it comes to diversity policies which define diversity along certain attributes and themselves contribute to differentiation processes, instead of focusing on the processes' social construction and addressing social inequalities and power relations that can stabilize them.

The concept of "just diversity" proposes that planners should be concerned with three interrelated social logics: redistribution (of resources and power), recognition (of diversity), and encounter (for increased sociality). It links procedural and substantial goals, is open for adaptation to different planning situations, and makes the decision-making process transparent. Planners are not neutral experts, but players in a political arena characterised by power relations and inequalities. Thus the concept puts individual planners in charge of designing the best procedure and at the same time responding to inequality and injustice (cf. Forester 2009). Planning is not or at least not primarily a technical discipline which can derive what to do from scientific knowledge. It is important to stress its political character and the individual responsibility of urban planners and policymakers. The awareness of the gender and diversity debates may be helpful to make individual positions and structural constraints visible and to reflect one's own position in the complex web of actors, identities and interests.

## References


Agyeman, J.; Sien Erickson, J. (2012): Culture, Recognition, and the Negotiation of Difference: Some Thoughts on Cultural Competency in Planning Education. In: Journal of Planning Education and Research, Vol. 32, pp. 358–366

Bauhardt, C. (2003): Equity Planning und Geschlechtergerechtigkeit. In: Planerin, No. 1, pp. 39–41 (in German)

Becker, R. (1992): Hat die Wohnungspolitik endlich die Alleinerziehenden entdeckt? In: Institut Wohnen und Umwelt (ed.): Gibt es Alternativen im sozialen Wohnungsbau? Anstöße aus frauenpolitischem Blickwinkel. Darmstadt a.o., pp. 82–96 (in German)

Becker. R. (1998): Zu kurz gesprungen? Anmerkungen zum vielschichtigen Unbehagen über den Stand feministischer Planung – Überlegungen zu einer Neuorientierung. In: Frei-Räume, Vol. 10, pp. 151–170 (in German)

Berg, M. Van den (2012): City Children and Genderfied Neighbourhoods: The New Generation as Urban Regeneration Strategy. In: International Journal of Urban and Regional Research, Vol. 49, No. 1, pp. 153–168

Bernt, M.; Fritsche, M. (2008): Kooperation – mit wem? Bewohnerbeteiligung im "Stadtumbau Ost". In: Vetter, A. (ed.): Erfolgsbedingungen lokaler Bürgerbeteiligung. Wiesbaden, pp. 237–258 (in German)

Blokland, T.; Van Eijk, G. (2010): Do People Who Like Diversity Practice Diversity in Neighbourhood Life? Neighbourhood Use and the Social Networks of "Diversity-Seekers" in a Mixed Neighbourhood in the Netherlands. In: Journal of Ethnic and Migration Studies, Vol. 36, No. 2, pp. 312–332

Bohle, P.; Falk, S.; Keller, K.; Kellermeyer, S.; Ott, Ch. (2004): Diversitätspolitik in Städten – Neue Wege der Integration. In: Wächter, H.; Führing, M. (eds.): Anwendungsfelder des Diversity Management. Munich a.o., pp. 189–260 (in German)

Bondi, L. (1991): Gender Division and Gentrification: A Critique. In: Transactions of the Institute of British Geographers, Vol. 16, No. 2, pp. 190–198

Bondi, L. (1999): Gender, Class and Gentrification: Enriching the Debate. In: Environment and Planning D: Society and Space, Vol. 17, pp. 261–282

Bridge, G.; Butler, T.; Lees, L. (ed.) (2012): Mixed Communities: Gentrification by Stealth? Bristol

Caglar, G. (2013): Gender Mainstreaming. In: Politics and Gender, Vol. 9, No. 3, pp. 336–344

Crouch, C. (2008): Postdemokratie. Frankfurt am Main (in German)

Davidoff, P. (1965): Advocacy and Pluralism in Panning. In: Journal of the American Institute of Planners, Vol. 11, No. 31, pp. 331–338

Dörhöfer, K., Terlinden, U. (1998): Verortungen. Geschlechterverhältnisse und Raumstrukturen. Basel a.o. (in German)

Fainstein, S. S. (2005): Feminism and Planning: Theoretical Issues. In: Fainstein, S. S.; Servon, L. J. (eds.): Gender and Planning. A Reader. New Brunswick a.o., pp. 120–138

Fainstein, S. S. (2010): The Just City. Ithaka

Fainstein, S. S.; Servon, L. J. (2005b): Introduction: The Intersection of Gender and Planning. In: Fainstein, S. S.; Servon, L. J. (eds.): Gender and Planning. A Reader. New Brunswick a.o., pp 1–14

Fainstein, S. S.; Servon, L. J. (eds.) (2005a): Gender and Planning. A Reader. New Brunswick a.o.

Fincher, R.; Iveson, K. (2008): Planning and Diversity in the City. Basingstoke a.o.

Florida, R. (2005): Cities and the Creative Class. New York

Forester, J. (2009): Dealing with Differences. Oxford

Frank, S. (2004): Feministische Stadtkritik. In: Häußermann, H.; Siebel, W. (eds.) Einführung in die Stadtsoziologie. Frankfurt am Main a.o., pp. 196–213 (with W. Siebel) (in German)

Frank, S. (2008): Gender Trouble in Paradise. Suburbia Reconsidered. In: DeSena, J. (ed.): Gender in an Urban World – Special Issue of Research in Urban Sociology. London, pp. 127–148

Greed, C. (2005): Overcoming the Factors Inhibiting the Mainstreaming of Gender into Spatial Planning Policy in the United Kingdom. In: Urban Studies, Vol. 42, No. 4, pp. 719–749

Hark, S. (2004): Lesbenforschung und Queer Theorie: Theoretische Konzepte, Entwicklungen und Korrespondenzen. In: Becker, R.; Kortendiek, B. (eds.): Handbuch Frauen- und Geschlechterforschung. Wiesbaden, pp. 104–111 (in German)

Hayden, D. (2002): Redesigning the American Dream: The Future of Housing, Work and Family Life. New York a.o.

Hayden, D. (2005): What Would a Nonsexist City Be Like? Speculations on Housing, Urban Design, and Human Work. In: Fainstein, S. S., Servon, L. J. (eds.): Gender and Planning. A Reader. New Brunswick a.o., pp. 47–64

Healey, P. (1992): Planning Through Debate: The Communicative Turn in Planning Theory. In: Town Planning Review, Vol. 63, No. 2, pp. 143–162

Huning, S. (2012): Open Spaces as Sites of Gender & Identity Construction – Implications for Open Space Planning. In: Gutiérrez Valdivia, B.; Cicoletto, A. (eds.): Estudios urbanos, género y feminismo – Teorías y experiencias. Barcelona, pp. 251–260

Huning, S. (2013): Ambivalences of Gender Planning. In: Metropolitics, 23.01.2013. – URL: http://www.metropolitiques.eu/Ambivalences-of-Gender-Planning.html

Huning, S. (2014): Wer plant für wen? Partizipation im Kontext gesellschaftlicher Differenzierung. In: Küpper, P.; Levin-Keitel, M.; Maus, F.; Müller, P.; Reimann, S.; Sondermann, M.; Stock, K.; Wiegand, Timm (eds.): Raumplanung 3.0 – Gemeinsam die Zukunft der räumlichen Planung gestalten. Hannover, pp. 33–43 (Working Reports of the ARL, No. 8) (in German)

Krumholz, N., Forester, J. (1990): Making Equity Planning Work. Philadelphia

Landry, C. (2000): The Creative City. A Toolkit for Urban Innovators. London

Reeves, D. (2011): Cross-cultural Communication: A Critical Competence for Planners. In: Planning Practice & Research, Vol. 26, No. 5, pp. 597–613

Roberts, M. (2013): Introduction: Concepts, Themes and Issues in a Gendered Approach to Planning. In: Sanchez de Madariaga, I.; Roberts, M. (eds.): Fair Shared Cities. The Impact of Gender Planning in Europe. Farnham, pp. 1–20

Rodenstein, M. (1998): Von der frauengerechten zur nicht-sexistischen Stadt. Ein Plädoyer für eine neue Perspektive in der feministischen Stadt- und Regionalplanung. In: Frei-Räume, Vol. 10, pp. 142–150 (in German)

Saldern, A. von (2004): Die Stadt und ihre Frauen. Ein Beitrag zur Gender-Geschichtsschreibung. In: Stadtraum und Geschlechterperspektiven. Informationen zur modernen Stadtgeschichte, No. 1, pp. 6–16 (in German)

Sandercock, L. (2000): When Strangers Become Neighbours: Managing Cities of Difference. In: Planning Theory & Practice, Vol. 1, No. 1, pp. 13–30

Sandercock, L. (2003): Out of the Closet: The Importance of Stories and Storytelling in Planning Practice. In: Planning Theory & Practice, Vol. 4, No. 1, pp. 11–28

Schuster, N. (2014): Diversity in der Stadtforschung – Einordnung und Kritik eines facettenreichen Konzepts. In: Altrock, U.; Huning, S.; Kuder, T.; Nuissl, H. (eds.): Zielgruppen in der räumlichen Planung. Konstruktionen, Strategien, Praxis. Berlin, pp. 25–50 (in German)

Smith, M. P. (2000): Transnational Urbanism: Locating Globalization. Oxford

Throgmorton, J. (2003): Planning as Persuasive Storytelling. In: Planning Theory, Vol. 2, No. 2, pp. 125–151

Turnhout, E.; Van Bommel, S.; Aarts, N. (2010): How Participation Creates Citizens: Participatory Governance as Performative Practice. In: Ecology and Society, Vol. 15, No. 4, Art. 26. – URL: http://www.ecologyandsociety.org/vol15/iss4/art26/

Vedder, G. (2006): Die historische Entwicklung von Diversity Management in den USA und in Deutschland. In: Krell, G.; Wächter, H. (eds.): Diversity Management – Impulse aus der Personalforschung, Munich a.o., pp. 1–23 (in German)

Wagner, T. (2013): Die Mitmachfalle. Bürgerbeteiligung als Herrschaftsinstrument. Köln (in German)

Waltz, V. (2014): Migranten und Migrantinnen im Blickfeld der Stadt- und Raumplanung. In: Altrock, U.; Huning, S.; Kuder, T.; Nuissl, H. (eds.): Zielgruppen in der räumlichen Planung. Konstruktionen, Strategien, Praxis. Berlin, pp. 167–182 (in German)

Wilson, E. (1991): The Sphinx in the City: Urban Life, the Control of Disorder, and Women. London

# eco-com.60+: Communal Living for the Elderly

## Ecological, Social and Economical Aspects

*Freya Brandl**

# 1 Introduction

Demographic change in Europe reflects an aging population. In Austria, an increasing number of the elderly in larger cities live alone in large dwellings (cf. Häberlein 2006). This results in unnecessarily high demand levels of not only energy, but also spatial and financial resources. Despite these circumstances, there is currently a lack of alternatives to living in conventional dwellings. There are indications that an increasing number of the elderly would prefer "living together apart", which means occupants spend a certain period of the day in their own spaces but part of the day is dedicated to communal living (cf. Durett 2009). In this context, the present paper explores the related topics of sustainability and energy efficiency for this population.

The hypothesized advantages of communal living models lie in the higher occupancy density as well as shared use of certain spatial resources. This paper explores this potential via numeric simulation. A communal living model is virtually integrated in existing houses in a specific district of Vienna and compared with conventional solutions. Moreover, this "densification" effect is both compared and combined with the energy efficiency effects of thermal retrofits of the respective buildings.

# 2 Method

## 2.1 Heating Load of Selected Objects

The $6^{th}$ district of Vienna was selected for this research: it is situated close to the center of the city and has an urban texture with an existing infrastructure (e.g. coffeehouses and restaurants, public transportation, shops, and cultural amenities). Furthermore, it has an aging population and a large building stock in need of retrofitting.

---

* A research project in cooperation with *Ardeshir Mahdavi* and *Kristina Kiesel*, Vienna University of Technology.

Two buildings of different construction periods were selected. Building "A" is a so-called "Gründerzeit-Haus", constructed around 1900/1910. The building has four stories and is about 20 m high. The external walls are made of common brick with a thickness of about 50 cm. The façade overlooking the street includes decorative features and is thus not suitable for thermal retrofit via external insulation. The apartments in this building type are relatively generous in size: the third floor, which is selected for the present study, contains three apartments with 80 $m^2$ to 130 $m^2$ net floor area (see Figure 1).

Figure 1: External View of Building A

Author's Archive

Building "B" is representative of buildings erected around 1950/1960. The building has six stories and two attic apartments, and is about 24 m high. The three upper stories were selected for the study, containing eight apartments with net floor areas (for each) ranging between 40 $m^2$ and 80 $m^2$ (see Figure 2).

Two occupancy models were considered: the first (individual) model which represents the current circumstances in many instances, assumes that a single occupant lives in each apartment. The second (communal) model assumes a higher occupancy via smaller individual apartments but involving shared (jointly used) areas. For each of these models, two sets of construction-related assumptions were considered: the first (existing) assumption denotes as-is construction features. The second assumption denotes thermally retrofitted constructions (see Table 1). For these four scenarios, (heating) energy demand was computed using a dynamic thermal simulation application (cf. EDSL 2011). Thus, the energy efficiency benefits of the communal living models could be compared with benefits associated with thermal retrofit measures. Table 2 gives a summary of the respective scenarios and the associated code. Note that in this table and the paper, the following abbreviations were used:

A: building A,
B: building B,
I: existing occupancy model (individual),
C: communal occupancy model,
E: existing thermal state of the buildings,
R: retrofitted thermal state of the buildings.

For example, B3_I_R denotes the third scenario for building B, individual occupancy model, thermally retrofitted.

Figure 2: External View of Building B

Author's Archive

Table 1: Overview of the Assumptions

| | *AS IS* | | *New* | |
|---|---|---|---|---|
| *Occupancy Model* | I | Individual | C | Communal |
| *Thermal State* | E | Existing | R | Retrofitted |

Author's Archive

Table 2: Simulation Scenarios for the Two Buildings with Respective Abbreviations

| *a* | *b* |
|---|---|
| A1_I_E | B1_I_E |
| A2_C_E | B2_C_E |
| A3_I_R | B3_I_R |
| A4_C_R | B4_C_R |

Author's Archive

Figures 3 and 4 illustrate the existing (individual) and the proposed (communal) occupancy models for building A respectively. Thereby, the existing three apartments are converted into five apartments: four single occupancy (net floor area around 50 $m^2$) and one double occupancy (72 $m^2$). Each apartment is equipped with a bathroom and a kitchenette. While the apartment sizes are smaller in the communal model, a relatively large space is provided for communal living including a living space with kitchenette and dining area, as well as a library or office room. Also some of the appliances are shared (washing machine, etc.).

Figure 3: Existing Floor Plan – Building A (individual)

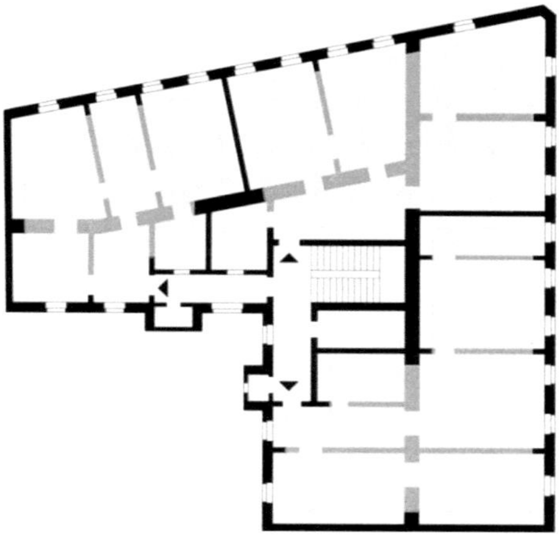

Author's Archive

Figure 4: Selected Floor in Building A – New Layout (communal)

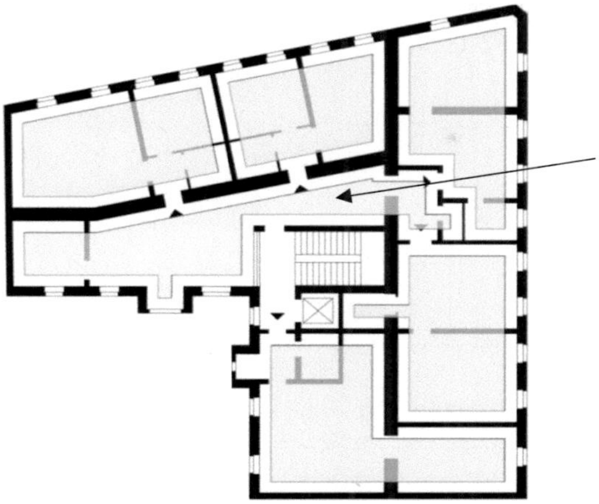

Author's Archive

Likewise, in the three selected floors of building B, instead of the existing eight apartments, ten smaller apartments (seven single and three double occupancy) are housed. Moreover, a shared living room including a kitchenette and a dining area, a library or office room, a guest room and a rooftop terrace have been implemented. Figures 5 to 8 show the corresponding individual and communal occupancy models. Assumptions pertaining to the two buildings and the two occupancy models are summarized in Table 3.

Figure 5: Existing Floor Plan – Building B, attic (individual)

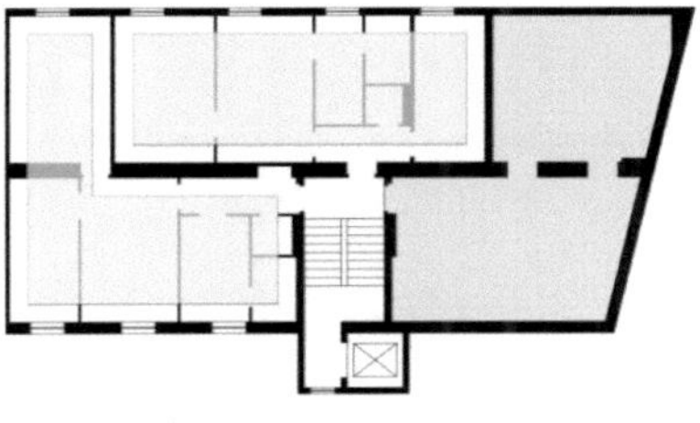

Author's Archive

Figure 6: Existing Floor Plan – Building B, 5th and 6th Floor (individual)

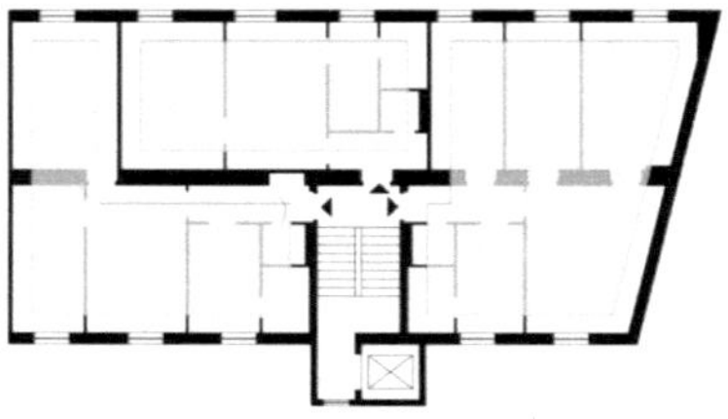

Author's Archive

Figure 7: New Layout – Building B, attic (communal)

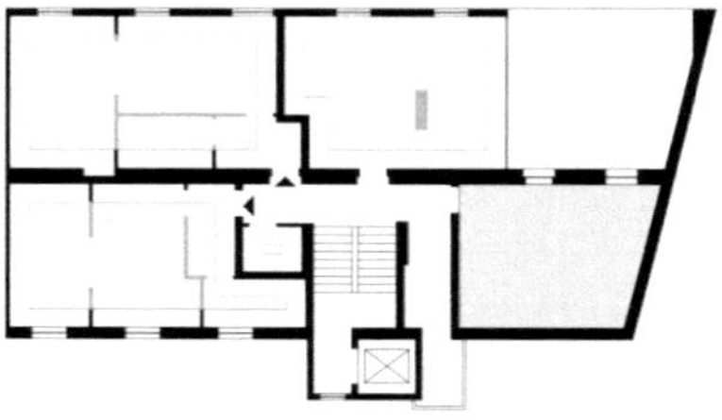

Author's Archive

Figure 8: New Layout – Building B, 5th and 6th Floor (communal)

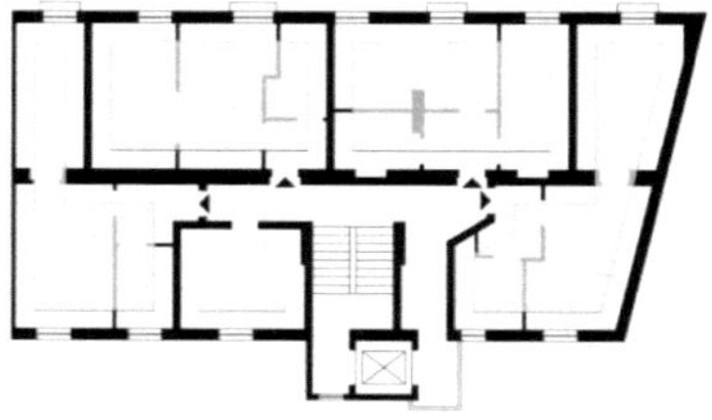

Author's Archive

The differences in the assumed occupancy conditions and processes between the individual and communal occupancy models result in corresponding simulation input assumptions regarding internal gains. These assumptions are summarized in Table 4.

Table 3: Summary Information on Simulated Objects

| | *Building* | | | |
|---|---|---|---|---|
| | *A* | | *B* | |
| | *I* | *C* | *I* | *C* |
| Floor height [m] | 3.30 | | 2.50 | |
| No. of apartments | 3 | 5 | 8 | 10 |
| No. of occupants | 3 | 6 | 8 | 13 |
| Net floor area [$m^2$] | 344 | 370 | 501 | 507 |
| Communal area [$m^2$] | – | 78 | – | 62 |
| Area per person [$m^2$] | 115 | 59 | 59 | 33 |

Author's Archive

Table 4: Assumed Internal Loads [$W.m^{-2}$]

| | | *A* | *B* |
|---|---|---|---|
| I | Occupancy | 0.63 | 1.23 |
| | Light | 0.85 | 1.61 |
| | Equipment | 2.07 | 4.01 |
| C | Occupancy | 1.18 | 2.18 |
| | Light | 1.22 | 1.59 |
| | Equipment | 3.57 | 5.75 |

Author's Archive

As mentioned before, buildings A and B are considered both in their present condition as well as after an assumed thermal retrofit. Thereby, exchange of windows and, where possible, improved thermal insulation of the external walls were taken into account. Table 5 provides an overview over the U-Value assumptions for the respective simulation models.

As the pertinent performance indicator, annual heating loads were calculated for both buildings. A standard weather file for Vienna was used (cf. Meteotest 2008). The computed heating loads were expressed either per net floor area of the dwellings or per occupant.

Table 5: U-Value Assumptions for Walls and Windows [W.m-².K-1]

| | A | | B | |
|---|---|---|---|---|
| | E | R | E | R |
| Ext. wall 20cm | 2.06 | 0.22 | | |
| Ext. wall 25cm | | | 1.79 | 0.25 |
| Ext. wall 38cm | | | 1.35 | 0.24 |
| Ext. wall 51cm | 1.10 | 0.39 | | |
| Int. wall 20cm | 2.11 | 0.27 | | 0.27 |
| Window frame | 2.06 | 1.10 | 2.06 | 1.10 |
| Window pane | 2.58 | 0.71 | 2.58 | 0.71 |

Author's Archive

## 2.2 Estimation of City-wide Energy Saving Potential

Subsequent to the simulation of the heating loads for the selected objects, an effort was made to roughly estimate the wider energy saving potential for the city of Vienna. The pertinent assumptions for this extrapolation exercise were as follows:

- Based on available data on the current age distribution of Vienna's population (cf. MA 2011), it can be estimated that, by the year 2035, approximately 600,000 people in the city of Vienna will be between 60 and 85 years old.
- It is conceivable that with appropriate information campaignes and policy measures, 10% of the above population (i.e., roughly 60,000 people) could be housed in communal living settings as opposed to individual dwellings. The occupancy density for these two options may be assumed to be 50 and 100 $m^2$ per person respectively, given an appropriate weighting of the information provided in Table 3.

# 3 Results

## 3.1 Heating Loads of the Selected Buildings

Tables 6 and 7 summarize the simulated heating loads (per $m^2$ net floor area and per occupant) for the two reference buildings (A, B) and the four scenarios (see Table 2). This information is shown in Figures 9 and 10 in relative terms, i.e. percentage reduction for scenarios 2 to 4 as compared to scenario 1.

Table 6: Heating Load for Building A

| | $kWh.m^{-2}.a^{-1}$ | $kWh.person^{-1}.a^{-1}$ |
|---|---|---|
| A1_I_E | 76.70 | 8,795 |
| A2_C_E | 61.54 | 3,802 |
| A3_I_R | 49.23 | 5,645 |
| A4_C_R | 34.77 | 2,150 |

Author's Archive

Table 7: Heating Load for Building B

| | $kWh.m^{-2}.a^{-1}$ | $kWh.person^{-1}.a^{-1}$ |
|---|---|---|
| B1_I_E | 87.38 | 5471 |
| B2_C_E | 76.56 | 2983 |
| B3_I_R | 19.82 | 1241 |
| B4_C_R | 16.78 | 654 |

Author's Archive

Figure 9: Reduction of the Heating Load per $m^2$ per Year Compared to the Existing Buildings [%]

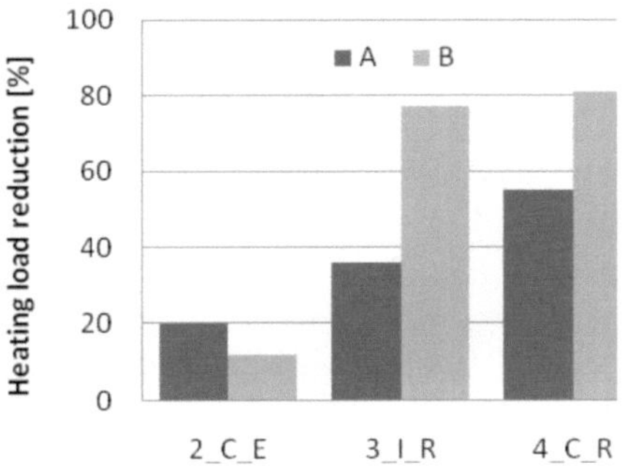


Author's Archive

Figure 10: Reduction of the Heating Load per Person and Year Compared to the Existing Buildings (%)

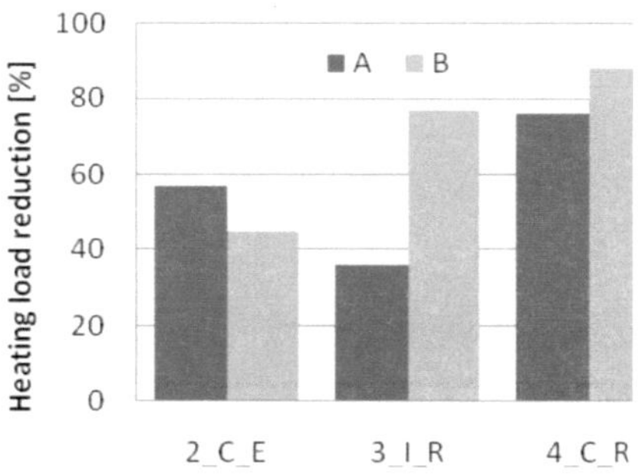


Author's Archive

## 3.2 Estimated City-level Heating Load Reduction

The estimated annual heating load reduction extrapolated to the entire city of Vienna would amount to 366 GWh, if by the year 2035 10% of the population in the age bracket 60 to 85 would be living in communal settings, instead of in single apartments. This corresponds to an estimated 77% reduction in heating energy use.

# 4 Discussion

## 4.1 Heating Load

The two instances of buildings selected for the present study (objects A and B) are not necessarily representative for all buildings in Vienna in strict statistical terms. Nonetheless, the situations they display (size, construction type, number of floors, etc.) are quite common. Thus, certain general inferences could be derived from their treatment in the above analysis, even though the introduction of communal living inadvertently results in changes in the total net floor areas of the apartments and the number of occupants (see Table 3).

The simulation results suggest that the thermal retrofit of the selected objects A and B (without introducing the communal living layout) would reduce the area-specific heating load by 36% and 77% respectively. The better result in the case of building B is due, in part, to the rather poor thermal characteristics of this building in its current state, as documented in Table 5. Moreover, the thermal insulation of the street-facing (decoratively articulated) external walls of building A could be only minimally improved.

Introduction of the communal living pattern without thermal retrofit would result in 20% and 12% heating load reductions in buildings A and B respectively. Both measures combined (thermal retrofit and communal living) would result in 55% and 81% heating load reductions. The energy efficiency effect of the communal living could be even more impressively illustrated if we consider heating load reductions per occupant. In that case, communal living (without thermal retrofit) would result in 57% and 45% heating load reductions for buildings A and B respectively. This implies that the per occupant energy efficiency improvement potential of the communal living scenario is comparable in magnitude with full thermal retrofitting of buildings. Obviously, the combination of both measures' results would represent the optimal solution. Thereby, heating loads could be reduced 55% and 81% (area-specific) or 76% and 88% (per occupant).

## 4.2 Additional Considerations

Our rough extrapolation of the above results on the urban scale for the city of Vienna points to a significant heating energy reduction potential. The estimated heating load reduction, if adjusted with a bulk factor of 0.3 for the efficiency of the heating systems, results in a delivered heating energy reduction of 520 GWh. Needless to say, aside from energy conservation, the communal living pattern would also bring about large savings in space usage (approximately 3 million square meters in terms of net floor area). This freed space could then be used for other occupants (families, young people, etc.) increasing thus not only space-use efficiency but also contributing to a more heterogenic (multi-generational) age structure. Our experience shows that, given proper architectural design, the reduction of area per occupant must not result in a loss of privacy or living quality. In fact, communal living has been shown to improve the life quality for many people.

Moreover, increased occupancy in the city proper would reduce urban sprawl and the associated rise in traffic and virgin land usage. Likewise, the existing infrastructure (e.g. shops, services, transportation) would be used more efficiently and the competitiveness of the inner district as a business location could be improved.

Aside from the calculated effects of such communal living models, there are additional benefits that appear feasible but are difficult to quantify:

- Communal living models bring people with different capabilities or disabilities together. In such groups, the potential for mutual support could reduce the need for interventions from outside and the associated energy and financial resources (e.g., for delivery and service trips).

- Increasing the occupancy density in the inner districts of the city makes it more convenient to participate in cultural and recreational activities. Places can be reached with public transport and if transportation services are needed, the distances are shorter (and the service can be used by more than one occupant at a time).
- Socially, the effects of such communal living models are manifold. Experiences with similar projects in different countries show that the groups grow together, regular group activities are organized, and the occupants feel less lonely and also much more secure, as they are surrounded by familiar people.

## References

Durett, C. (2009): The Senior Cohousing Handbook – A Community Approach to Independent Living. Gabriola Island, Canada

EDSL (2011): A-TAS Version 9.2.1. Environmental Design Solutions Limited. – URL: www.edsl.net

Häberlein, U. W. (2006): Lebens- & Wohnformen – Singles in Wien. Entwicklung zur Privatheit und Funktionalisierung der Räume. In: Beiträge zur Stadtentwicklung, Nr. 04 (MA 18, Stadtentwicklung und Stadtplanung). – URL: https://www.wien.gv.at/stadtentwicklung/studien/pdf/b008042.pdf [May 2011] (in German)

Magistrat der Stadt Wien (2011): Bevölkerung nach Altersgruppen und Staatsangehörigkeit 2006 bis 2008. Wien (MA 05, Stadt Wien. Vienna, Austria). – URL: www.wien.gv.at/statistik/bevoelkerung/demographie/bevoelkerungszusammensetzung.html [May 2011] (in German)

Meteotest (2008): Meteonorm Version 6.1. – URL: www.meteonorm.com

# 4. Sustainable Universities

katja saar

# Making the Campus Sustainable

## The Example of the Catholic University of Eichstaett-Ingolstadt

*Ingrid Hemmer, Péter Bagoly-Simó*

## 1 Introduction

What does sustainable development look like at universities? What is the current status of its implementation in Germany? Which factors promote it and which difficulties arise in the individual contexts? These are some of the main questions this paper dedicates special attention to. In doing so, the focus is on the Catholic University of Eichstaett-Ingolstadt.

## 2 Universities and Their Contribution to Sustainable Development

Formal, informal, and non-formal education have been embracing concepts of sustainable development for decades. Chapter 36 of the global Agenda 21 stresses the importance of education for the process of general transformation towards more sustainable societies. Despite its clear focus on the K-12 stages of formal education, Chapter 36 also sets a framework for higher education (cf. BMUNR 1992). According to the document, universities should work and teach following the principles of (Education for) Sustainable Development (ESD). In the wake of the Earth Summit, several international, regional, and national charters and declarations on (E)SD in higher education were signed. Among the most relevant ones are the Copernicus Charter (1994), the Thessaloniki Declaration (1997), the Lueneburg Declaration (2001), and the Lucerne Declaration on Geographical Education for Sustainable Development (2007). Ratified two years after the Earth Summit, the Copernicus Charter (1994) set ten principles of action on the agenda of institutions of higher education: institutional commitment, environmental ethics, education of university employees, programs in Environmental Education (EE), interdisciplinary approaches, dissemination of knowledge, networking, partnership, life-long learning programs, and technology transfer. Fifteen years after the 1992 Rio Summit, geographers from around the globe gathered in Lucerne to develop a core declaration to foster the implementation of (E)SD into formal geography education.

Comparing institutions of higher education on a regional scale shows that the most visible progress in the area of (E)SD implementation among German universities has been achieved so far at the Leuphana University of Lueneburg. Several other universities, such as the Eberhard-Karls University of Tuebingen, the University of Bremen, and the University of Hamburg made the first steps to become more sustainable.

Along with pioneers like the Leuphana University of Lüneburg, the Sustainable University of Applied Sciences Eberswalde, and the Birkenfeld Campus of the University of Trier, the Catholic University of Eichstaett-Ingolstadt is the only university in Bavaria adopting a resolute institution-wide approach, one of the four most important measures in the United Nations' Global Action Programme, the UN's follow-up initiative to the Decade of Education for Sustainable Development (UNDESD) (cf. UNESCO 2013). A whole-institution approach consisting of research, education, and campus management proved to be the most efficient way to achieve the goal of universities becoming social role models. Thereby, research and education are the two dimensions that strongly interact and lead to synergies. However, a corresponding (re-)design of campus management according to the principles of (E)SD is indispensable to live up to their own standards of sustainability (see Figure 1). In the following, the Catholic University of Eichstaett-Ingolstadt serves as an example to illustrate how the institution-wide approach is put into practice.

## 3 The Catholic University Eichstaett-Ingolstadt: Becoming a More Sustainable University

The implementation of (E)SD can follow different paths. In many cases, however, implementation is a result of a mixture of bottom-up and top-down strategies (cf. Nickolaus/Graesel 2006). This is the case for the Catholic University of Eichstaett-Ingolstadt.

Three years after the Earth Summit, student initiatives started promoting SD at an institutional level. Among the most significant actions were (guest) lecture series that aimed at raising awareness among students, faculty, and staff. One of the most important results of this action was the introduction of the concept of SD both at the institutional level and within different departments. Consequently, the bottom-up initiatives produced a paper demanding a stronger discussion of SD at the Catholic University of Eichstaett-Ingolstadt. In spite of the fact that the institution had already signed the University Charter for Sustainable Development within the Copernicus-Program as early as 1994, university administration during the mid-1990s was less willing to dedicate more attention to SD. As a consequence, students carried out all initiatives (e.g. the continuation of the guest lectures about environmental and sustainability issues) aiming at making the university more sustainable. Over the 2000s the initiatives experienced a progressive decay, until SD was reintroduced in 2008 on the university's agenda. Once again, student initiatives were of central relevance. Members of the Student Council for Environmental Issues restarted the guest lecture series and created the "Sustainable Campus" project, an award-winning initiative at the national competition "Generation D". Within this initiative, recommendations like the use of recycled-paper or fair trade products sold at the cafeterias were put into practice. Additional initiatives, such as the use of solar energy on campus, are still being discussed.

Figure 1: Development of (E)SD at the Catholic University of Eichstaett-Ingolstadt

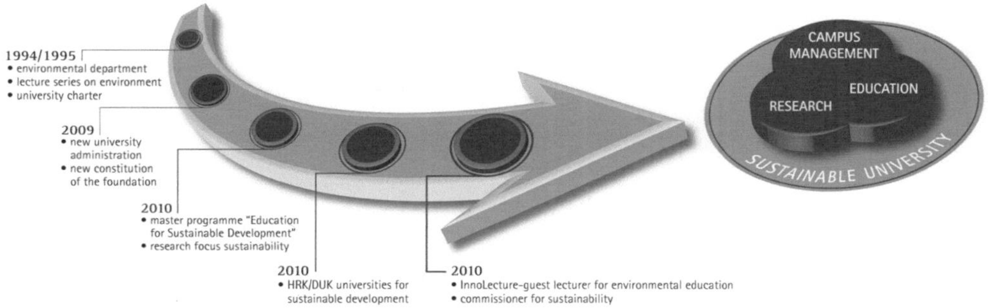


Source: modified after Hemmer et al. 2012, p. 14

The revival of student-driven bottom-up initiatives at the end of the last decade came along with major changes at the level of university administration. Starting with 2008, sustainability was even included in the institution's new constitution (*Stiftungsverfassung*) and became a more important issue in all relevant areas, namely education, research, and campus management. Regarding education, courses started discussing sustainability following an interdisciplinary approach. In addition, a new Master of Science program "Geography: Education for Sustainable Development" started in fall 2010. Research about SD also became more central as different research programs with an emphasis on sustainability topics were launched.

The Declaration of German Rectors and the German UNESCO Commission "Universities for Sustainable Development" offered the strongest support to these initial achievements. Moreover, an InnoLecture Guest Lectureship in EE funded by the Foundation for German Science and the newly introduced position of ESD-Commissioner in 2010 further nurtured (E)SD at the Catholic University. Student initiatives coming from different departments and subjects also reinforced past bottom-up support. As a consequence, in late 2010 the university administration released the institutional Sustainability Strategy. The document aims to contribute to SD by means of three main areas: education, research, and campus management. Figure 1 summarizes the most important steps and players during the last two decades.

# 4 Awareness Level and Acceptance of the New Overall Concept

Unlike past bottom-up actions, several recent decisions regarding (E)SD were implemented in a top-down manner. In addition, some of these decisions had reduced visibility and effects on education and life on campus. Therefore, it was of great importance to explore the visibility and acceptance of the new overall concepts among students and faculty.

## 4.1 Methods and Sample

To map the diffusion and acceptance of the new overall concept of the university, an exploratory survey was carried out in June-July 2011. The sample consisted of 42 students aged 21–30 (14 male, 26 female) in their $4^{th}$ to $9^{th}$ semester majoring in Geography and German with Latin, English, French or History as minors. Most respondents were enrolled in teacher training programs at bachelor level with an emphasis on primary or secondary education.

Data was collected by means of a questionnaire. Throughout the sampling, assistance was offered by student helpers. The questionnaire surveyed prior knowledge on the concept of SD, awareness of the new overall concept of sustainability, and options to increase awareness. Rebecca Schwenk and Simone Krummer carried out data collection and preparation as part of their seminar activity within the module Sustainable Development in the summer semester of 2011.

## 4.2 Results

The results show that most students possess prior knowledge on one or more aspects of sustainable development. Mapping prior knowledge was based on an open question asking respondents to name three concepts related to sustainable development. Geography students named – in order of frequency – the dimensions (ecological, economical, and social) of sustainability, followed by the concept of future, and resource and environmental preservation. Students majoring in German placed environmental preservation on the top of their list. Resource preservation counted second, while the third named concept showed some heterogeneity: education, future, growth, and stability. Thus, future geographers think in terms of sustainable development, while future philologists (still) stress the aspect of natural conservation.

Another item asked respondents to give a definition of sustainable development. Results reflect the same discrepancy described above. For most Geography students sustainable development is "[r]esource consumption in a way that enables future generations to enjoy them. This happens on ecological, economical, and social bases". In addition, some respondents also pointed out aspects of "social, economic, and ecological equity/justice". Students majoring in German conceptualized sustainable development as a way to "shape the future in a lucrative and environmentally sound manner". However, according to other respondents, sustainable development is "[m]easured use of resources to make sure that following generations have something too". In contrast to their fellow students, German majors added (again) an educational dimension: sustainable development is "long-term and future-oriented education and research". In spite of this conceptual and definitional diversity, not all respondents were able to define sustainable development. Geography majors (76.19%) did somewhat better in comparison with students majoring in German (66%).

Participants who defined sustainable development were asked in the subsequent item to rank the importance of the concept on a scale from 1 (very important) to 5 (not important at all). Both groups of respondents displayed the highest frequency counts on value 2 (important). In contrast, students majoring in Geography displayed the second-highest frequency counts on very important (value 1), whereas German majors opted in the second-most cases for neither important nor unimportant (value 3).

The fourth category of items explored the visibility and perception of the university's overall concept of sustainable development. Almost twice as many Geography majors (86%) were familiar with the overall concept as their fellow students majoring in German (43%). However, some differences in the degree of familiarity need to be addressed. More than half of all participants (57%) were marginally familiar with the concept and an additional 14% had only a rough idea of it. A quarter of all respondents were not familiar with the decision of the Catholic University regarding sustainability initiative changes. While twice as many Geography majors had a rough idea of the overall concept as German majors, two times more German majors were not familiar at all with the new concept as compared to Geography students. Only three per cent of all respondents were familiar with the details of the new overall concept.

When asked to name possible solutions for improved visibility for the new overall concept, students offered a wide range of solutions. High on the agenda of both Geography and German majors was online visibility (e.g., the institution's main homepage). According to the respondents, the new overall concept needs stronger visibility by being placed on the homepage. Further, Geography students suggested an integration of the new overall concept into elements of corporate design, specifically the university logo. Students majoring in German considered information points and information days as the important actions that could be taken to improve visibility. On the top three list of what can be done, Geography majors placed implementation of sustainable development into educational offerings (courses and seminars) in third place. Courses were on rank three in the top 3 of German majors also, along with flyers, stronger public relations work, and posters.

Students also had suggestions regarding the implementation of sustainable development into everyday life on campus. Geography majors named posters, (guest) lectures, changes in educational offerings, field trips, and also direct steps such as the use of energy from renewable sources (specifically electricity) or waste separation around campus. Students majoring in German also suggested general actions such as (guest) lectures, posters, changes in the educational offerings. In more specific terms, they also pointed out the usefulness of workshops and projects directly related to sustainable development. Another suggestion given by several respondents was to offer best practice examples within the (guest) lectures. Regarding campus management, the Catholic University could use recycled paper, reduce overall paper consumption, and a switch to solar energy.

## 4.3 Discussion

The exploratory survey revealed various aspects of the way students perceive the implementation of sustainable development at the Catholic University of Eichstaett-Ingolstadt.

Most Geography majors defined sustainable development according to the triple-pole model but also stressed aspects of intra- and intergenerational equity/justice. In contrast, German majors complemented the concept of sustainable development with an educational dimension. These results can be explained on one hand by the affinity of the geographical sciences with the triple-pole model of sustainability and, on the other hand, by the stronger affinity of German literature and linguistics with the professional requirements of future teachers. For the latter group, sustainable development often manifests itself in a practical way, such as waste management or paper recycling, whereas Geography majors appear to grasp the larger conceptual dimension in part through their academic training.

Both student groups expressed personal interest for the university's new overall concept. In spite of their different backgrounds, most students only marginally reflected awareness of the changes in the overall concept. The higher familiarity of Geography students with certain aspects of changes on the university level is due to the localization of early initiatives and the recent support for a more sustainable university in the Faculty of Mathematics and Geography, especially within the geography chairs.

Faculty actively involved in the new overall concept directly implemented changes into their educational activities.

Suggestions regarding higher visibility, better acceptance, and more successful implementation of the new overall concept covered two of the three main areas (education, research, and campus management) of sustainable development at the Catholic University of Eichstaett-Ingolstadt.

Concerning education, students expressed their wish to learn more about sustainable development in two main ways. First, sustainability aspects should be implemented into their subject-related training. While this aims at a broad coverage of sustainability in all training programs, the challenge lies in the research and teaching autonomy of faculty. Further, some subjects might encounter difficulties in implementing sustainable development into their respective programs. Second, a general (guest) lecture series and workshops could complement subject-related higher education, meeting individual preferences and needs. While this suggestion probably is an easier (initial) way of implementing a new overall concept, it might also reflect students' reluctance to accept compulsory modules on sustainability as part of their graduation requirements.

Campus management is the second main areas covered by students' suggestions. Several aspects mentioned in the questionnaires emerge from individual every-day experiences of un-sustainability on campus. Waste separation is, for example, not solved by far. Further, waste management remains a challenge for the entire institution. Renewable sources of energy, specifically solar energy, were on the top of many of the respondents' agendas. This strong emphasis on electricity, however, might be a direct cause of the ongoing debate on the nuclear power phase-out in Germany. A stronger control of paper consumption along with alternative sources, such as recycled paper, was mainly on the agenda of German majors. This is probably strongly subject-related and a consequence of the degree of digitization of management, administration, and teaching.

# 5 The Realization of the Overall Concept from 2012 to 2014

A new university administration was elected in the fall of 2011. While overall progress continued, certain areas of the overall concept reached a phase of stagnation. Concerning research, the Sustainability Graduate School, which was founded in 2010, continued its work. In addition, several new and large research projects with a focus on sustainable development started at the campus in Eichstaett (e.g. SuMaRiO-Sustainable Management of River Oases along the Tarim River). An international conference of more than a hundred participants was held in Eichstaett at the end of 2012.

This conference brought together young scientists who presented and discussed their postgraduate and Ph.D. projects from different fields of (E)SD. Additionally, keynote addresses given by well-known scientists highlighted critical aspects of past development and outlined perspectives for the future (cf. Müller et al. 2014). First steps to establish an interdisciplinary Research Institute for Sustainability were made, however, organizational and institutional decision is still pending.

Regarding education, several departments, especially Geography, Social Work, Psychology and Economics, opted to include sustainable development and ESD into their educational offerings. The interdisciplinary module "Sustainable Development", which was created as a facultative module in 2011, has received the status of an elective module in a growing number of programs. Demand is still considerable. There are ambitions to integrate sustainability with two other fields into Studium generale, which would result in one third of the students at the Catholic University being familiar with sustainability. However, stronger networking and evaluation within and among the individual departments is still pending. An award for the best thesis in the field of sustainability was handed out for the first time in November 2014.

Regarding campus management, the process of preparation for the EU Eco-Management and Audit Scheme (EMAS) certification started in 2011. Within this process the executive board identified and defined fourteen measures (including waste and energy management, and also reporting on the implementation status of sustainable development) to be taken by the end of 2014. The process accelerated thanks to the support of the university's new chancellor, elected in 2012, who opened a position for campus management. Although not included in the overall concept, bottom-up initiatives coming from administrative staff created a program in which the Catholic University has improved green electricity use since January 1st, 2012. Additionally, a solar power system was installed on the roof of the cafeteria. Along these lines, two Sustainability Reports for the years 2012 (cf. Hemmer et al. 2013) and 2013 (cf. Hemmer et al. 2014) were published. Students participated in the creation of both reports. The report of the Catholic University of Eichstaett-Ingolstadt compared well to sixteen reports from other universities. Nonetheless, a need for improvement was also revealed (cf. Sassen et al. 2014). The efforts over the recent years were rewarded in fall 2013 when the sustainability concept was awarded the distinction of "UN-Decade Project".

The Plan for Structure and Development of the Catholic University of Eichstaett-Ingolstadt was released in early 2014. Much effort by the commissioner for sustainability was necessary to integrate sustainability as an element of both profile and field of action. However, higher-clarity statements at some points could have been desirable. Students and their well-established participation in the concept including bottom-up initiatives such as "The Day of Eco-Social Market Economy", the Dialogue on Sustainability, waste programmes, clothing exchange parties, and many more were vital elements of the development of a more sustainable university.

# 6 Networks and Cooperation

## 6.1 The International and National Scale

The Catholic University of Eichstaett-Ingolstadt supports and organizes various activities in different fields for both national and international networking and cooperation. One example comes from the Chair of German Language and Literature Education. The chairwoman provided five students from the teacher-training program with the opportunity to do an internship in Uganda. This has resulted in a long-term partnership and a return visit that is expected to take place in the near future. Another example comes from the Professorship of Geography Education. As parts of field trips to Switzerland in 2012 and Austria and Hungary in 2014, students had the opportunity to have close encounters with protagonists in the field of sustainability including representatives from the Universities of Berne, Graz and Vienna. The commissioner for sustainability is very active in various committees of the UNDESD on a national level, in particular the working group "Universities and Sustainability" that supported the sustainability initiatives at the Catholic University of Eichstaett-Ingolstadt.

## 6.2 The Regional and Local Scale

The Catholic University of Eichstaett-Ingolstadt is part of several networks in Bavaria, for example the Round Table for Education for Sustainable Development within the Bavarian Ministry for Environment. Together with the Munich University of Applied Sciences, the Catholic University initiated the Bavarian network of "Universities for Sustainable Development", which is a regional section of the national working-group "Universities and Sustainability", and aims at promoting the rather reluctant implementation of (E)SD at Bavarian universities. For this action, the Catholic University and its partners were awarded the distinction UN-Decade-Measure (cf. DUK 2014, p. 14). Moreover, the Catholic University also cooperates on a regional and local level with the working-group "Nature and Environmental Education ANU e.V.", the diocese of Eichstaett, the Bavarian "Centers for Environmental Education", the One World Initiatives, and the city of Eichstaett on its development as a Fair Trade City. Despite the interest and opportunities for cooperation, scarce human resources impede further networking on the regional and local scale.

# 7 Factors Promoting Implementation and Challenges

Summarizing the implementation achievements on the overall concept over the last four years, the Catholic University of Eichstaett-Ingolstadt has taken a considerable step towards becoming a more sustainable university. A range of factors contributed to this process (see Figure 2). Of central importance was, among others, the synergy between bottom-up and top-down initiatives and measures, the great support of the university administration in 2008, one to two dozen engaged faculty, administrative staff continuously verbalizing their concerns and needs, and two active student groups who kept the subject on the agendas of various stakeholders.

Figure 2: Implementation of the Whole-institution Approach of the Catholic University of Eichstaett-Ingolstadt

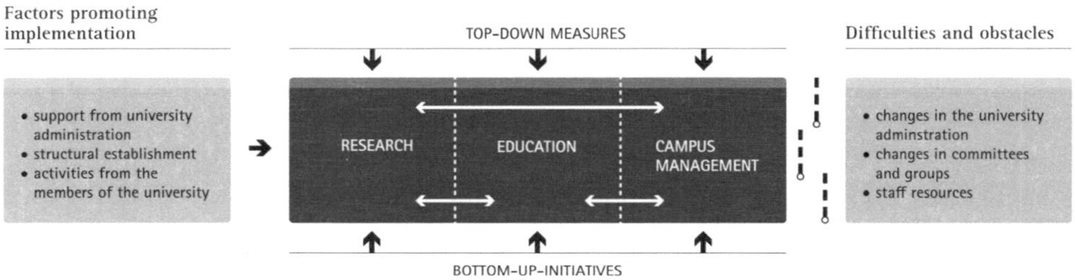


Authors' Archive

Strong promotion of sustainability undoubtedly influenced the consideration of (E)SD issues in the institution's new constitution (*Stiftungsverfassung*), the whole concept of sustainability, the process of EMAS-certification, the appointment of a commissioner for sustainability, the opening of a position for campus management, and the appointment of the chancellor as responsible party for sustainability matters with the university administration.

Challenges arose because of two changes in the university administration between 2010 and 2014 resulting in poor and slow decision-making. Furthermore, steady changes in committees and student groups led to the necessity to popularize the university's overall concept of sustainable development over and over. Finally, the number of participants who put significant effort into this concept is still very limited, since working for a more sustainable university is still voluntary and translates into an additional workload to one's regular tasks, as exemplified by the activities of the commissioner for sustainability. Thus, the most important factor limiting activities are shortcomings in human resources.

# 8 Prospects

From a current perspective, the Catholic University of Eichstaett-Ingolstadt will continue its journey to become a more sustainable university. Once again, a change in university administration must be optimized. It would be desirable to transform the Catholic University of Eichstaett-Ingolstadt in particular and institutions of higher education in general into engines of sustainable development for regions and cities. Transdisciplinary projects already taking place today need to be reinforced, particularly in terms of human resources. Financial and human resources seem to be the key factors to not only enable universities to become aware of their responsibilities, but also to fulfil their commitment.

## References

BMUNR – Bundesministerium für Umwelt, Naturschutz und Reaktorsicherheit (1992): Umweltpolitik. Agenda 21. Köln/Bonn (in German)

DUK – Deutsche UNESCO-Kommission (ed.) (2012): Hochschulen für eine nachhaltige Entwicklung. Nachhaltigkeit in Forschung, Lehre und Betrieb einer Hochschule. Bonn (in German)

DUK – Deutsche UNESCO-Kommission (ed.) (2013): Hochschulen für eine nachhaltige Entwicklung. Ideen zur Institutionalisierung und Implementierung. Bonn (in German)

DUK – Deutsche UNESCO-Kommission (ed.) (2014): Hochschulen für eine nachhaltige Entwicklung. Netzwerke fördern, Bewusstsein verbreiten. Bonn (in German)

Hemmer, I.; Bagoly-Simó, P.; Zirkl, F. (2011): Die Katholische Universitaet Eichstaett-Ingolstadt auf dem Weg zu einer nachhaltigen Hochschule. In: Böttger, H.; Gien, G., Pitroff, Th. (eds.): Aufbrüche. Eichstaett, pp. 10–21 (in German)

Hemmer, I.; Japha, V.; Krajewski, Ns. (2013): Nachhaltigkeitsbericht 2012. Katholische Universitaet Eichstaett-Ingolstadt. Eichstaett (in German)

Hemmer, I.; Baumann, J.; Niggemeyer, S. (2014): Nachhaltigkeitsbericht 2013. Katholische Universitaet Eichstaett Ingolstadt. Eichstaett (in German)

Müller, M.; Hemmer, I.; Trappe, M. (eds.) (2014): Nachhaltigkeit neu denken. Rio+x: Impulse für Bildung und Wissenschaft. München (in German)

Nickolaus, R.; Graesel, C. (eds.) (2006): Innovation und Transfer – Expertisen zur Transferforschung. Hohengehren (in German)

Sassen, R.; Dienes, D.; Beth, C. (2014): Nachhaltigkeitsberichterstattung deutscher Hochschulen. In: ZfU – Zeitschrift für Umweltpolitik & Umweltrecht, Vol. 37, No. 3, pp. 258–277 (in German)

UNESCO – United Nations Educational, Scientific and Cultural Organization (2013): Proposal for a Global Action Programme on Education for Sustainable Development as Follow-up to the United Nations Decade of Education for Sustainable Development (DESD) After 2014. Paris

# Applied Sustainability Education with a Systems Science Emphasis at a STEM University

*Kenyon C. Lindeman*

## 1 Introduction

Universities have a historic and continuous role as urban centers of education, research, and the arts: they are explicit lynchpins of culturally and technologically strong cities and societies. A fundamental university role at local through international scales is the development of innovations in any number of human endeavors (cf. Cortese 2003; Aber et al. 2009; Calder/Dautremont-Smith 2009). Gregory Trencher, Masaru Yarime, Kes B. McCormick, Christopher N. Doll and Stephen B. Kraines provide evidence for an "… emerging, new mission for the university", where universities provide unique resources to local government, industry and NGOs to advance sustainable transformations of cities or regions (cf. Trencher et al. 2014). Over time, the impacts of such innovations (technological or social or both) feed back into academic curricula with the emergence of new courses and programs reflected in expanded sustainable practices on campus and beyond (cf. Sterling/Huckle 2014).

In support of the evolving role of universities and innovation, high school students in the U.S. are displaying an increased interest in sustainability degree programs and careers (cf. AASHE 2009; Chronicle of Higher Education, 2010; Princeton Review 2015). For example, over 100 major, minor, and certificate programs were created in 2009 on energy- and sustainability-focused programs in the U.S. (cf. Schmit 2009). More than 25% of incoming freshmen considered "becoming involved in programs to clean up the environment" as essential or very important (cf. Chronicle of Higher Education 2010), an increase of > 50% from five years prior. A survey of 16,000 students and parents found that 66% were interested in college sustainability efforts and 24% said such information would "very much" impact application or attendance decisions (cf. Princeton Review 2011).

A survey of 260 U.S. university administrators on the availability of "interdisciplinary environmental degrees" included the term sustainability and concluded "the last two decades have seen extraordinary growth in the creation of new educational programs" (Vincent 2009). Note that these programs often include sustainability certifications and specializations. Minor and major academic programs are also increasing in occurrence but require more resources. University sustainability programs of many varieties can work to integrate academics and campus operations (cf. Parnell et al. 2014) and research (cf. McMillin 2009).

The steady increase in the national interest in sustainability is reflected in the increases in university bachelors degree offerings, with over 70 B.S. or B.A. degree titles including the term *sustainability* available in the U.S., the majority appearing since 2000. University investments in sustainability are based in part on employer demand for interdisciplinary systems thinkers, the competitive advantages of increased student recruitment, the potential for reduced operating costs and the desire to innovate (cf. Princeton Review 2015).

Many sustainability degrees are Bachelor of Arts and are not at institutions that historically specialize in Science, Technology, Engineering, and Mathematics (STEM) content areas. Adjacent to NASA's Kennedy Space Center in coastal east Florida, Florida Institute of Technology (F.I.T.) began new academic sustainability initiatives in 2010 which imbedded work on campus and community best practices. A minor program began in Fall 2010 and a Bachelor of Science major in 2013/14 that introduced new courses specific to system science and sustainability, and project design and management, in addition to > 100 interdisciplinary elective courses. Over two thirds of the undergraduate population at F.I.T. are in the College of Engineering or College of Science. STEM universities offering named sustainability bachelors degrees are not common but include Rensselaer Polytechnic Institute and Rochester Institute of Technology in the northeastern U.S.

In Florida and the southeast U.S., the Sustainability Studies bachelors program at F.I.T. is one of the first of its type among STEM universities. A preliminary case study is constructed here from recent initiatives at this university with a focus on:

(a) the diversity of interests among academic programs in differing colleges,
(b) the use of system sciences in sustainability education, and
(c) campus and community green initiatives as curricular objectives.

Primary program development trends are considered with a focus on optimizing responses to system complexities that arise when building university sustainability initiatives.

# 2 Academic Sustainability

## 2.1 Sustainability Programs

At least 72 U.S. universities offer bachelors degrees with the words *Sustainable* or *Sustainability* in the degree title. 43 of these degrees are B.S. and 29 are B.A. based on reviews conducted in through early 2014. The most common degree titles include Sustainability Studies, Environmental Sustainability, and Sustainable Development. Many degree titles also reflect specific disciplines such as Sustainable Business or Sustainable Agriculture. Sustainability Studies degrees are offered in both B.S. and B.A. programs. Online sustainability majors, certificates, and specializations are also offered by some U.S. universities. At least 50 foreign universities offer bachelor-equivalent sustainability degrees in various languages via on-site or online programs.

Of almost 100 colleges and universities in Florida, < 25% currently have formal minor programs in sustainability, and < 10% have named majors in sustainability. There are various certificates and specializations in sustainability and related fields in Florida colleges and universities as elsewhere. The numbers of these types of programs can be sizeable compared to formal major and minor academic programs which are recorded on final transcripts.

The initiation of a Sustainability Minor program in 2010 and a Bachelor of Science in Sustainability Studies major program in 2013 at F.I.T. have added four new courses specific to sustainability, systems science, and green project design to date. Interdisciplinary courses from four concentration categories are also required for the minor and major programs: Business, Environmental Sciences, Technology and Engineering, and Social Sciences. Cross-campus integration of sustainability into other programs is advanced by a sustainability module within the University Experience course required of freshmen in all majors and a University Sustainability Council with multiple faculty representatives from all colleges and primary administrative departments on campus.

Between academic years (AY) 2010/11 and 2014/15, over 60 students graduated with a minor in sustainability (see Figure 1). By the end of AY 2015/16, over 80 students total will have graduated with the minor or the new major (AY 2015/16 data is projected from Dec. 2015 petition-to-graduate paperwork). Overall, 25% of the total graduates are from outside of the U.S. with 12 total countries represented and six graduates each from India and the Middle East. Since AY 2010/11, the program has steadily attracted more students with 20 or more students graduating in three of the last four academic years, with the highest numbers in the last two years (see Figure 1). This is more than two times the next most popular minors on campus, of 30 total minor programs at F.I.T.

A major attribute of the sustainability minor program is the diversity of different majors represented in the student population. Figure 2 shows the total number of graduates from each college for the first six academic years. Students from over 20 different majors from the five colleges on campus will have earned the sustainability minor by the end of AY 2015/16. The College of Engineering will have the highest number of graduates to date with 38 students (see Figure 2). The College of Science will have 24 graduates during this period. The Colleges of Business, Psychology and Liberal Arts, and Aeronautics will have 12, 5, and 3 graduates, respectively, by the end of AY 2015/2016.

Figure 1: Graduation Totals by Year for the Sustainability Minor and Major Programs, Academic Years 2010/11–2015/16, Florida Institute of Technology

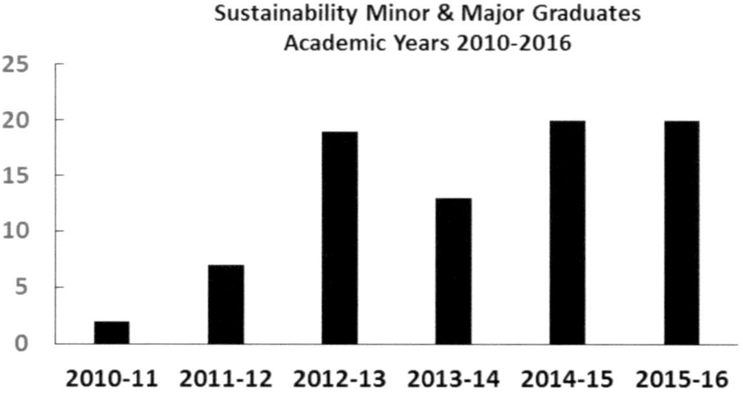


Author's Archive

Figure 2: Graduation Totals by College for Sustainability Minors and Majors, F.I.T., Academic Years 2010/11–2015/16

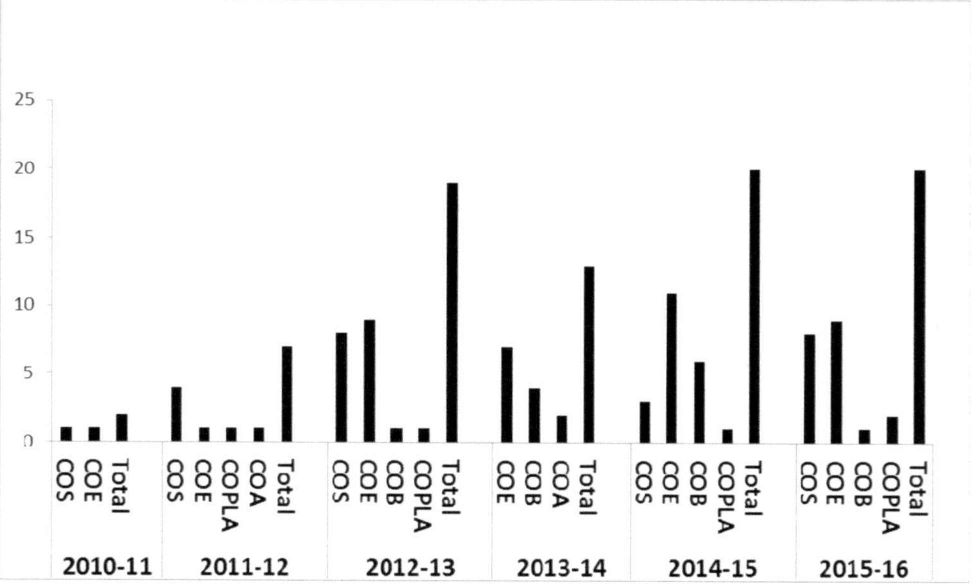


COS: College of Science
COE: College of Engineering
COPLA: College of Psychology and Liberal Arts
COB: College of Business
COA: College of Aeronautics

Author's Archive

The 38 graduates from the College of Engineering are represented by ten majors (see Figure 3). The majority of these students, 15, are from the Construction Management program. The Department of Marine and Environmental Systems is represented by 10 total sustainability minors, from Environmental Science, Ocean Engineering, and Oceanography majors (5, 3, and 2 graduates, respectively). The Civil Engineering and Mechanical Engineering majors had 7 and 2 sustainability minors, respectively. In an important reflection of the continued dispersal of inter-disciplinary sustainability at

Figure 3: Graduation Totals for Sustainability Minors, College of Engineering, F.I.T. Academic Years 2010/11–2015/2016

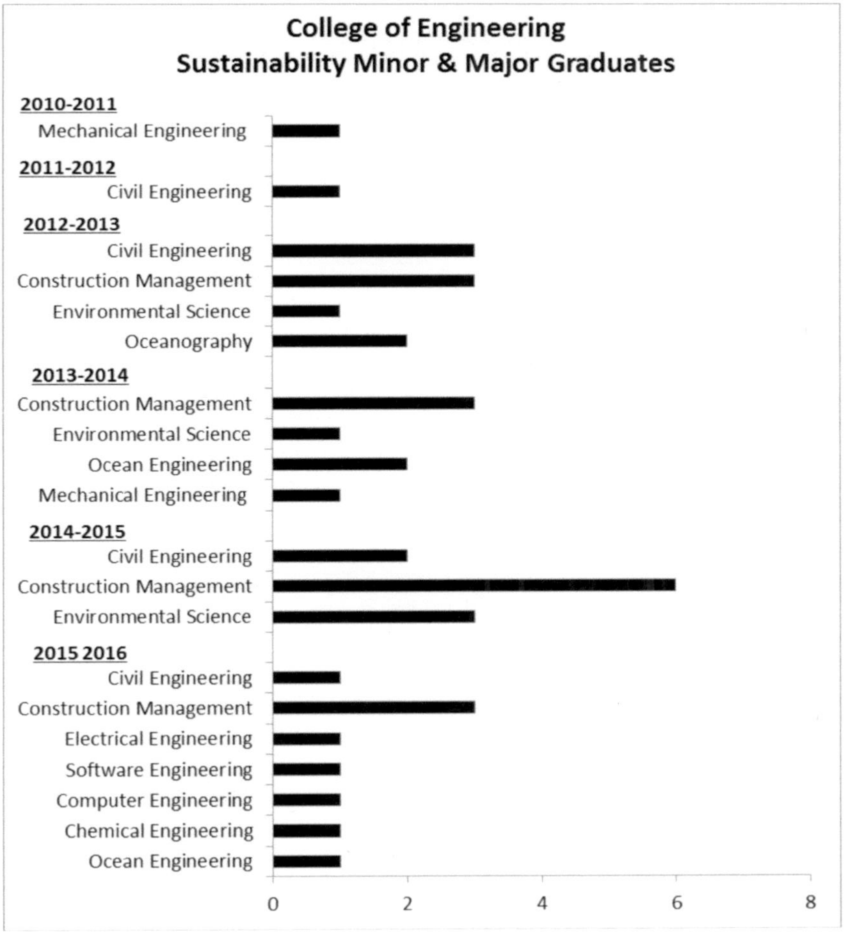


Author's Archive

F.I.T., four new engineering majors will have their first sustainability minor graduates in AY 2015/16: Electrical Engineering, Computer Engineering, Software Engineering, and Chemical Engineering.

Based on pending data, the College of Science will have three major programs with sustainability minor graduates by the end of AY 2015/16. Over the history of the program, fourteen graduates are from the Marine Biology major (see Figure 4). Five minor graduates are from the Interdisciplinary Science major, with an additional one from the Premedical Biology major. The 12 sustainability graduates from the Nathan M. Bisk College of Business comprise several specializations from that College's recently re-organized undergraduate program structure including Global Business, Marketing, Business and Environmental Studies, and Accounting. Major programs in the College of Psychology and Liberal Arts that had sustainability minor graduates included Communications, Humanities, and Forensic Psychology majors.

Figure 4: Graduation Totals for Sustainability Minors and Majors, College of Science, F.I.T. Academic Years 2010/11–2015/2016

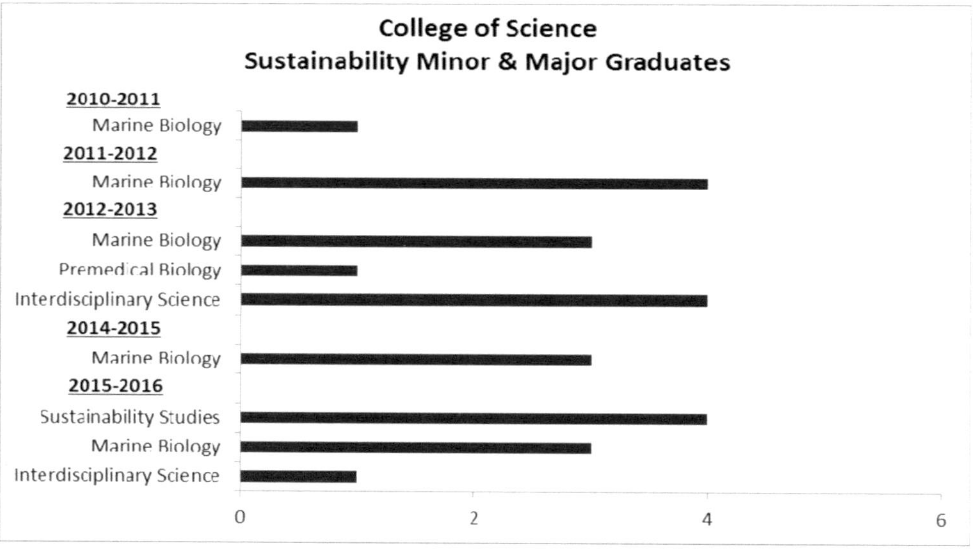


Author's Archive

Based on the results from the minor program and scoping of the growing number of U.S. universities with bachelors programs in sustainability (cf. Princeton, Review, 2011), F.I.T. launched a Bachelor of Science program in Sustainability Studies in Fall 2013. The first graduate of the new major program was in Dec 2015, with 3 more students graduating by the end of AY 2015/16 (see Figure 4). The program curriculum takes advantage of F.I.T.'s existing STEM strengths and includes two years of core science preparation with one year each required of calculus, physics, chemistry and biology (all courses are 4, not 3, credit hours including laboratory components). Juniors and seniors have > 100 intermediate and advanced sustainability elective courses available including a range of economics and social sciences courses to enhance the transfer of science and technology innovations into corporate and government realms. In total, Sustainability Studies majors take a minimum of 6 economics/business courses and up to 12 courses in some cases.

## 2.2 Systems Science Education for Sustainability

To further examine hierarchical system dynamics within and among natural, social, and economic capital, additional sustainability courses have been launched with more in development. The emphasis includes systems sciences and green project management with new upper level courses such as Systems, Governance and Sustainability (ISC 3250) and Sustainable Project Design (ISC 3999). The prerequisite for both of these courses is Introduction to Sustainability (ISC 1500) which uses "Thinking in Systems: A Primer" (cf. Meadows 2008) as a textbook to introduce systems complexity and sustainability using stock-flow dynamics and feedback to explain non-linear networks and long-term system behaviors. Approximately 160 students from > 20 majors and all F.I.T. colleges have taken this course through AY 2015/16.

The applied academic goals in ISC 1500 are to learn and explore combinations of tools that advance innovations in sustainability among complex socio-economic and environmental systems. The introductory focus is on five interconnected mega-systems developed from class notes that drive most of the Earth's most challenging sustainability issues: Population and Consumerism; Natural Capital and Biodiversity; Energy and Climate; Economics and Business; and Communications and Societal Dialogue, collectively the Five Guerillas.

Primary components of systems science in ISC 1500 include stocks and flows, feedback loops, limits, response delays, orderly and chaotic perturbations, system traps, shifting dominance of feedback, tipping points, and post-transition system behaviors. At intermediate levels in ISC 3250, tools such as complexity theory, risk-based decision assessment, resiliency, behavioral economics, political ecology, and social network analysis are detailed (cf. Espinoza/Walke 2011). Practical applications in real-world political systems are emphasized at local through international scales (cf. Lindeman et al. 2015; Worldwatch Institute 2014).

Collectively, best practices in maintaining complex systems through non-equilibrium processes for long term sustainability are examined in integrated courses and through applied projects. Means to identify, measure, adapt and communicate performance indicators of sustainability are queried and compared among government, business, and non-profit systems. The management of emergent properties and other guaranteed surprises is illustrated using resilience science applied to economic, environmental, and social capital examples (cf. Walker/Salt 2006).

# 3 Campus and Community Sustainability

For both minors and majors in sustainability, the required junior/senior capstone projects use a campus and community classroom model: students develop and manage applied sustainability projects on campus or in the larger city- or county-scale community for applied project management experience. In fall 2014, ISC 3999, a one-credit Sustainable Project Design course, became a prerequisite for the three-credit ISC 4000 for minor students and an original requirement in the major program. Student/staff/faculty teams have worked on issues including campus recycling, LEED building certification, composting, sustainable events, off-campus internships, and major planning processes such as the first campus sustainable transportation plan, stormwater plan, green IT plan, and sustainable purchasing plan. The addition in summer 2015 of a new University Sustainability Office (USO) in Facilities Operations will assist and expand many campus initiatives.

Capstone course projects are structured to generate interdisciplinary and team learning experiences (see Figure 5) and include:

- *Sustainable Buildings:* Many students have implemented best practices in building systems with senior Facilities Operations staff and consultants via work on U.S. Green Building Council certification credits. Many minor students doing building projects were majors in Construction Management and Civil Engineering but some were from diverse majors in the Colleges of Business and Science. Students have worked on all credit categories for LEED certification: Sustainable Sites, Water Efficiency, Energy and Atmosphere, Materials and Resources, Indoor Environmental Quality, and Innovation. With Facilities staff, this collaboration has helped result in the certification of one LEED Silver building, an outdoor campus swimming complex with new energy and water efficiency design features, and two other LEED buildings, one Certified and one potential Gold. All three of these buildings were evaluated in the New Construction category.
- *Recycling:* Student projects have included dormitory, electronics, and workspace recycling. Planning for more fully integrated projects is being aided by the USO, the Office of Residence Life and staff in specific areas (e.g. the campus library). Best practices will be reinforced by design and implementation of signage with effective messaging by the USO and other Facilities resources, student organizations and the Marketing Office.

Figure 5: Campus and Community Sustainability Groups (Circles) Associated with Applied Sustainability Course Capstone Projects (Boxes), 2012–14, F.I.T.

Black: Student Teams; White: Student Projects

Author's Archive

- *Dining Services:* Further expansion of organic and vegan dining options, new cardboard baler systems, more certified sustainable coffee options, more recycled packaging, sourcing of food waste for composting, and cooking oil to power university vehicles are among the projects undergoing scoping or implementation for on-campus dining options.
- *Land & Water:* Garden clean-ups and invasive plant removal in F.I.T.'s 16 acre Botanical Gardens and wetland are managed by Facilities Operations and aided by on- and off-campus organizations. Enhanced signage on the importance of this watershed to the larger City of Melbourne for stormwater runoff and other functions is being scoped. Students and staff have maintained a vermiform composting system at intervals using waste from the dining hall of the Student Union Building. Rainwater gardens and other stormwater innovations are also being scoped.

- *Sustainable Events:* Diverse best practices in sustainability are increasingly used in event management. Students have worked to bring sustainable practices to campus offices and events including the F.I.T. Conference Services Bureau, International Festival, Woman's Business Center, and campus Botanical Festival. Students have also worked to bring best practices in sustainability to very large off-campus events including several years of the Melbourne Music Marathon and Ron-Jon's Beach and Board Festival in Cocoa Beach with many thousands of attendees per event.
- *Community Internships:* F.I.T. students have done internships with local non-profit organizations for their capstone projects since AY 2011/12. These include multi-year partnerships with NGOs, businesses and governments such as Keep Brevard Beautiful, Smooth Running, and the City of Satellite Beach, respectively. Interns have worked on several initiatives for a major regional watershed NGO, the Marine Resources Council, including the 2014 American Assembly for the Indian River Lagoon, the lagoon health report card, and a green lagoon business certification program.
- *Sustainability Communications:* Messaging and education are fundamental to adoption of best practices for many projects. In the past, student groups, the SGA, and university staff offices have distributed sustainability information across multiple outlets to tell some of the stories that underlie making new sustainability projects sustainable. These efforts are now coordinated largely by the Communications Subcommittee of the University Sustainability Council and other resources.

# 4 Discussion

The first two students to enter the sustainability minor program were majors in Mechanical Engineering and Marine Biology; fitting as these are the two largest majors in the College of Engineering and College of Science at F.I.T. Total minor graduates for AY 2016/17 are conservatively estimated at between 25 and 30, the highest graduate totals to date. The class of May 2017 will exceed 100 total major and minor graduates since AY 2010/11.

It is often said that sustainability is a process and not an end; this certainly applies to the early stages of academic program creation and implementation (cf. Sharp 2002). There are various applied goals and projects that will still take many years to make operational on campus. One priority is expanded integration of sustainability education across academic programs on campus. A sustainability module has been added to the University Experience course required of all freshmen. Over 500 freshman participate in this course annually.

The large Northrup Grumman Design Showcase at F.I.T. in 2013 was won by a team of Construction Management students, three of these four students were also in the Sustainability minor program. The first Sustainability UnderGraduate Academic Research competition (SUGAR) occurred within the 2015 Northrup Grumman Showcase, with the winning project being an internship report on an indicator-based report card on the status of the Indian River Lagoon, a major Florida estuary. Business and Psychology students also presented research on campus vehicle GHG emissions and coastal climate adaptation at SUGAR 2015.

The creation of the new University Sustainability Office will be valuable to numerous facets of campus sustainability including a major focus on energy, water and waste efficiencies. In addition, the University Sustainability Council (USC) with 24 current members is explicitly increasing coordination among staff, faculty and students to advance best practices across the Florida Tech campus. Representatives include senior staff from diverse campus offices, faculty members from all colleges, and student representatives. Broad objectives include:

- Create a forum to plan, resource, and implement best practices in sustainability across academic curricula, campus operations and community outreach.
- Assist development of measurement protocols for campus sustainability systems including GHG emission inventories and energy management, building performance, recycling, and others.
- Coordinate the development of trans-disciplinary curricula in sustainability studies across all colleges.
- Increase performance in best practices following Princeton Review's Guide to Green Colleges, AASHE's Sustainability Tracking and Rating System (STARS), LEED building rankings, and other measures.

The U.S. Bureau of Labor Statistics does not have direct data on the number of workers involved in sustainability activities but there is widespread evidence of increasing opportunities for workers trained in a diverse array of sustainability-related position (cf. Hamilton 2012; Princeton Review 2015). The Economic Policy Institute examined in 2012 the private and public sector markets for sustainability-related jobs with these conclusions: greener industries grow faster, states with more developed sustainability policies fared better in the economic downturn, green jobs go far beyond renewable energy, and manufacturing plays a strong role in the green economy (cf. Pollack 2012).

In terms of those doing the hiring, one of the largest studies on CEO opinions of sustainability, Peter Lacy, Tim Cooper, Rob Hayward and Lisa Neuberger surveyed > 700 CEOs and the conclusions imply an increasing demand for sustainability-trained workers (cf. Lacey et al 2010):

- 93% of CEOs believe that sustainability issues will be critical to the future success of their business.

- 91% of CEOs report that their company will employ new technologies to address sustainability issues over the next five years.
- 96% of CEOs believe that sustainability issues should be fully integrated into the strategy and operations of a company (72% in 2007).

The new Sustainability Studies major program at F.I.T., the fourth named bachelors program to date in the state of Florida (with > 80 colleges and universities total), will have its first graduate in the fall semester of 2015. Though still in early stages, the program is catalyzing deeper levels of interdisciplinary study and applied systems science within the structure of the university's five colleges. We anticipate further advances in interdisciplinary education and sustainability research to be catalyzed by the major and minor academic programs, the USO, the USC, and many other campus and community partners. There are few reasons to conclude that interest in academic and campus sustainability will decline in the near future (cf. earlier citations). The evidence suggests that coordinated sustainability programs at STEM universities can also integrate economics and social sciences to advance interdisciplinary innovations in research and application on campuses and far beyond.

## Acknowledgements

The first waves of sustainability students at Florida Tech have been at the center of all academic, campus and community progress. Diverse students have helped drive the courses, enact new green projects, and aid new planning. Morgan Wilson, Lucy Gogin-Muns, and Bryce Beard aided this study. Many other students have contributed to sustainability at Florida Tech. Diverse staff around campus in various offices have assisted including Greg Tsark, Rob Ghiotto, Daniel Sutton, and Holly Chichester of Facilities Operations. Many faculty have also aided program start-up, particularly Gordon Nelson, Rich Aronson, Tom Marcinkowski, Laszlo Baksay, Kastro Hamed, and Hamid Rassoul and Michael Grace of the College of Science Dean's office. The support of Mark Craddock and Siemens Engineering for the continuing sustainability conferences is acknowledged. The German hosts for this meeting, as the Hungarian hosts for prior meetings, were outstanding and deserve our gratitude for their work.

## References

AASHE – Association for the Advancement of Sustainability in Higher Education. (2009): Green Majors Growing in U.S. Schools. Dec 29. – URL: www.aashe.org

Aber, J.; Kelly, T.; Mallory, B. (eds.) (2009): The Sustainable Learning Community. One University's Journey to the Future. New Hampshire

Calder, W.; Dautremont-Smith, J. (2009): Higher Education: More and More Laboratories for Inventing a Sustainable Future. In: Dernbach, J. (ed.): Agenda for a Sustainable America. Washington, D.C. (Environmental Law Institute), pp. 93–107

Chronicle of Higher Education. (2010): The Year's Freshmen at 4-year Colleges: Highlights of a Survey. Jan 21. – URL: http://chronicle.com/article/This-Years-Freshmen-at-4-Year/63672/

Cortese, A. (2003): The Critical Role of Higher Education in Creating a Sustainable Future. In: Planning for Higher Education, Vol. 31, No. 3, pp. 15–22

Espinosa, A.; Walke, J. (2011): A Complexity Approach to Sustainability: Theory and Application. London

Hamilton, J. (2012): Is a Sustainability Career on Your Green Horizon? Washington, D.C. (US Bureau of Labor Statistics) August (Report 7). – URL: http://www.bls.gov/green/sustainability/sustainability.pdf

Lacy, P.; Cooper, T.; Hayward, R.; Neuberger, L. (2010): A New Era of Sustainability. UN Global Compact-Accenture CEO Study 2010. Washington (Accenture) June (United Nations Global Compact). – URL: http://www.accenture.com/sitecollectiondocuments/pdf/accenture_a_new_era_of_sustainability_ceo_study.pdf

Lindeman, K. C.; Dame, L. E.; Avenarius, C. B.; Horton, B. P,; Donnelly, J. P.; Corbett, D. R.; Kemp, A. C.; Lane, P.; Mann, M. E.; Peltier, W. R. (2015): Science Needs for Sea-Level Adaptation Planning: Comparisons among Three U.S. Atlantic Coastal Regions. In: Coastal Management. Vol. 43, No. 5, pp 555–574

McMillin, J. (2009): Developing a Whole-of-university Approach to Educating for Sustainability Linking Curriculum, Research and Sustainable Campus Operations. In: Journal of Education for Sustainable Development, Vol. 3, No. 1, pp. 55–64

Meadows, D. H. (2008): Thinking in Systems: A Primer. White River Junction, VT

Parnell, R.; Berutich, L.; Henn, A; Koressel, N. (2014): The Campus as a Four-year Undergraduate Learning Laboratory on Sustainability: Linking Facilities, Operations, Curriculum, and Community Engagement. In: Council on Undergraduate Research Quarterly, Vol. 35, No. 1, pp. 11–19

Pollack, E. (2012): Counting up to Green: Assessing the Green Economy and its Implications for Growth and Equity. Washington, D.C. (Economic Policy Institute) (Briefing Paper #349). – URL: http://s4.epi.org/files/2012/bp349-assessing-the-green-economy.pdf

Princeton Review (2011): College Hopes and Worries Survey. – URL: http://www.princetonreview.com/college-hopes-worries.aspx

Princeton Review (2015): Princeton Review Guide to 353 Green Colleges. Princeton

Schmit, J. (2009): As Colleges Add Green Majors and Minors, Classes Fill Up. In: USA Today, Dec 28. – URL: http://usatoday30.usatoday.com/money/industries/environment/2009-12-27-green-colleges_n.htm

Sharp, L. (2002): Green Campuses: The Road from Little Victories to Systemic Transformation. In: International Journal of Sustainability in Higher Education, Vol. 3, No. 2, pp. 128–145

Sterling S.; Huckle, J. (2014): Education for Sustainability. Abingdon

Trencher, G.; Yarime, M.; McCormick, K. B.; Doll, C. N.; Kraines, S. B. (2014): Beyond the Third Mission: Exploring the Emerging University Function of Co-Creation for Sustainability, Science and Public Policy, Vol. 41, No. 2, pp.151–179

Vincent, S. (2009): Growth in Environmental Studies and Science Programs. In: Association for Environmental Studies and Sciences, Vol. 2, No. 2, pp. 1–4

Walker, B; Salt, D. (2006): Resilience Thinking: Sustaining Ecosystems and People in a Changing World. Washington, D.C.

Worldwatch Institute. (2014): Governing for Sustainability: State of the World 2014. Washington, D.C.

# Authors

*Albiez, Marius;* Dipl.-Geoökol.; Karlsruhe Institute of Technology (KIT), Institute of Technology Assessment and Systems Analysis (ITAS), Karlsruhe, Germany; marius.albiez@kit.edu

*Bagoly-Simó, Peter;* Professor Dr.; Humboldt-University of Berlin, Chair of Didactics of Geography, Berlin, Germany; peter.bagoly-simo@geo.hu-berlin.de

*Balouktsi, Maria;* M.Sc.; Karlsruhe Institute of Technology, Centre for Real Estate, Karlsruhe, Germany; maria.balouktsi@kit.edu

*Banse, Gerhard;* Professor Dr.; Karlsruhe Institute of Technology (KIT), Institute of Technology Assessment and Systems Analysis, Karlsruhe (ITAS) // Berlin Centre Technology & Culture, Berlin, Germany; gerhard.banse@partner.kit.edu

*Brandl, Freya;* Arch. Dipl.-Ing. Dr. techn.; Vienna University of Technology, Institute of Architectural Sciences, Vienna, Austria; freya.brandl@tuwien.ac.at

*Damodaran, Appukuttan;* Professor Dr.; Indian Institute of Management Bangalore, Economics & Social Sciences Area, Bangalore, India; damodaran@iimb.ernet.in

*Geiger, Albert;* City Administration, Head of the Unit Sustainable Urban Development, Ludwigsburg, Germany; a.geiger@ludwigsburg.de

*Gothe, Kerstin;* Professor Dr.; Karlsruhe Institute of Technology (KIT), Institute of Design of City and Landscape, Karlsruhe, Germany; kerstin.gothe@kit.edu

*Grunwald, Armin;* Professor Dr.; Karlsruhe Institute of Technology (KIT), Head of Institute of Technology Assessment and Systems Analysis (ITAS), Karlsruhe, Germany; armin.grunwald@kit.edu

*Haldar, Tanushree;* cand. PhD; Indian Institute of Management Bangalore, Bangalore, India; tanushree.haldar@iimb.ernet.in

*Hemmer, Ingrid;* Professor Dr.; Catholic University Eichstaett-Ingolstadt, Department of Didactics of Geography, Eichstätt, Germany; ingrid.hemmer@ku.de

*Huning, Sandra;* Dr.-Ing.; Dortmund University of Technology, Department of Urban and Regional Sociology, Dortmund, Germany; sandra.huning@tu-dortmund.de

*Lindeman, Kenyon C.*; Professor Dr.; Florida Institute of Technology (FIT), Melbourne, FL, U.S.; lindeman@fit.edu

*Lützkendorf, Thomas;* Professor Dr.-Ing.; Karlsruhe Institute of Technology, Centre for Real Estate, Karlsruhe, Germany; thomas.luetzkendorf@kit.edu

*Meyer-Soylu, Sarah;* Dipl.-Geooekol.; Karlsruhe Institute of Technology (KIT), Institute of Technology Assessment and Systems Analysis (ITAS), Karlsruhe, Germany; sarah.meyer@kit.edu

*Parodi, Oliver;* Dr.; Karlsruhe Institute of Technology (KIT), Institute of Technology Assessment and Systems Analysis (ITAS), Karlsruhe, Germany; oliver.parodi@kit.edu

*Quint, Alexandra;* M.Sc.-Geogr.; Karlsruhe Institute of Technology (KIT), Institute of Technology Assessment and Systems Analysis (ITAS), Karlsruhe, Germany; alexandra.quint@kit.edu

*Szypulski, Anja;* Dr.; Dortmund University of Technology, Department of Urban- and Regional Sociology, Dortmund, Germany; anja.szypulski@tu-dortmund.de

*Tulbure, Ildiko;* Assoc.-Prof. Dr.-Ing.; University "1 December 1918", Alba Iulia, Romania // Clausthal University of Technology, Clausthal-Zellerfeld, Germany; ildiko.tulbure@tu-clausthal.de

*Waitz, Colette;* Dipl.-Umweltwiss.; Karlsruhe Institute of Technology (KIT), Institute of Technology Assessment and Systems Analysis (ITAS), Karlsruhe, Germany; colette.waitz@kit.edu